Living in the
LAST GENERATION

Fred DeRuvo

Living in the Last Generation

Copyright © 2011 by Study-Grow-Know

All rights reserved. Written permission must be secured from the publisher to use or reproduce any part of this book, except brief quotations in critical reviews or articles.

Published in Scotts Valley, California, by Study-Grow-Know
www.studygrowknow.com • www.adroitpublications.com

Scripture quotations, unless otherwise noted, are from The Holy Bible, King James Version. This version is in the public domain.

Images used in this publication (unless otherwise noted) are from clipartconnection.com and used with permission, ©2007 JUPITERIMAGES, and its licensors. All rights reserved.

Any Woodcuts used herein are in the Public Domain and free of copyright.

All Figure illustrations used in this book were created by the author (unless otherwise noted) and protected under copyright laws, © 2011.

Cover Design and Interior Layout: Fred DeRuvo

Edited by: Hannah Richards

Library of Congress Cataloging-in-Publication Data

DeRuvo, Fred, 1957 –

ISBN 0977424405
EAN-13 9780977424405

1. Religion – Eschatology

Contents

Foreword	5
Chapter 1: Olivet Discourse	9
Chapter 2: Three Questions	18
Chapter 3: Birth Pangs	26
Chapter 4: After the Birth Pangs	51
Chapter 5: It's an Abomination!	62
Chapter 6: Run Away! Flee!	71
Chapter 7: Inside North Korea	78
Chapter 8: Hell Breaks Loose	89
Chapter 9: A Break in the Action	97
Chapter 10: No Guessing Please	105
Chapter 11: Hypocrisy	116
Chapter 12: What About You?	119

"He which testifieth these things saith, Surely I come quickly. Amen. Even so, come, Lord Jesus. The grace of our Lord Jesus Christ be with you all. Amen."

– Revelation 22:20-21 (KJV)

• FOREWORD •

With so many people asking questions about what is going on in the world, and with people stating unequivocally the day that Jesus will be returning, it makes you wonder if it is possible to know the truth at all. That answer depends upon what the *source* is for truth.

Too many people today take the word of someone else - someone who only *seems* to have more authority than they do - to determine the truthfulness of something. This, of course, does not mean that we should not listen to the expressed opinions of people who are experts in their field. However, it *does* mean that we should weigh any evidence carefully before coming to a conclusion.

Take the case of Harold Camping and his recent revelation that says Jesus is coming back to this earth on May 21, 2011. Is that information true? We know two things about it that will help us determine the truthfulness of Camping's claim.

1. Jesus said no one will know the day or hour of His return (cf. Matthew 24:35-37)
2. Jesus *could* return on that day, but if so, it would be a lucky guess on Camping's part

Why is it people like Harold Camping can make these bold statements that claim a specific time of Jesus' return when in point of fact Jesus Himself said no one would know the day or hour? Obviously, since Camping has picked out the date of May 21, 2011 as the day of Jesus' return, then Camping is guilty of disagreeing with Jesus. Camping is actually doing far more than that, however. He is actually calling Jesus a *liar*, something Jesus is not by any stretch.

Of course, we know that Camping is not the only individual who has claimed to know when Jesus would be returning. Most who know anything of church history know that decades ago the Millerites (the precursor to Seventh-day Adventism) stood on a hill in white robes waiting for Jesus' return. They were understandably very disappointed when His physical return did *not* occur.

Joseph Smith of Mormonism also pointed to a time when Jesus would return. That did not happen either.

Others like Ellen G. White (the original head of Seventh-day Adventism) also pointed to specific times when Jesus was to return, and when it did not happen as they said it would, it was simply pointed out that Jesus *had* come back, but *invisibly*. People who call themselves Preterists believe the same thing about A.D. 70. They believe that when Jerusalem and the Temple were destroyed by the Romans, that was God judging Israel and Jesus "came back" invisibly to do so. It is hard to disprove someone's charge that Jesus returned invisibly; however, one is forced to ask why Jesus would need to return invisibly when He is already here invisibly.

Jesus does *not* need to come back to be in control of all that occurs on this planet. He rules from heaven's throne. However, my belief is that Jesus *will* return one day in fulfillment of a variety of promises and He will return *physically*, so that every eye will see Him, just as He said He would (cf. Matthew 24:30, Mark 13:26).

It is difficult to take Jesus' words and turn them into something else entirely, yet this is what people have been doing ever since He walked on this planet. Either He actually meant that no one would know the day or hour, or He meant something else. When He spoke those words, He was not - if context means anything - speaking in allegory. He was speaking clearly, plainly, and distinctly at a time when He knew His death was soon to occur.

Jesus had taken the time to warn and instruct His apostles and disciples of things that would happen as this age draws to a close. Because of that, He did not couch His words with hidden meaning. He provided clear instruction and expected His listeners to understand His meaning as He meant it.

So what about all the claims that are heard today by numerous individuals? Whether it is a guy with a Foghorn Leghorn voice known as Harold Camping announcing to the world that he knows the day when Jesus is returning, or Apollo C. Quiboloy of the Philippines claiming to actually *be* Jesus Christ, there must be a way to know for sure what, if any, truth these and others are claiming.

There *is* a way, and the only way that I know of is to find the truth in the Bible. The problem is that either people constantly rip things out of context, or they do not want to trust the Bible for a variety of reasons.

Many see the Bible as fallacious because *other people* have told them that it is filled with contradictions, or that it was written by human beings who made mistakes. Those mistakes were passed down from generation to generation and additional mistakes and inaccuracies were added to the mix.

That is certainly a *convenient* way to avoid having to read the Bible for one's self, but the truth is that unless people take the time to personally investigate these negative claims about the Bible, they will never get to a point where they ever feel comfortable with the Bible.

This book is a commentary of sorts on one part of the Bible; the Olivet Discourse. This has got to be one of the most important messages that Jesus left us with because it outlines what is to happen *before* it happens. This is one of the most important aspects of the Bible. It contains many passages that were/are specifically *prophetic* in nature.

This is God's way of saying that because He tells us something in many cases *long before the events occur*, this speaks to His truthfulness and veracity. He goes out of His way to alert us to events way ahead of time in order that we will believe in Him *because* of those events. Unfortunately, many people are either unaware of those events, or choose not to believe them even when the evidence points back to Him.

In the Olivet Discourse, Jesus prophetically points to certain events; something He calls *birth pangs*. Not only can we determine *what* those birth pangs are, but whether or not they *have* occurred at all.

If at least some of them have occurred, then it is logical to assume that others will occur as well. What good does it possibly do to take the word of a friend or even a pastor or teacher, if you are unwilling to do the research yourself to determine the veracity of Jesus' claims?

What I have tried to do in this book is to present the evidence Jesus provides for when He says the last days, or end times, will be here. I have attempted to provide additional information outside the Bible to see whether or not Jesus is correct.

I hope that these cogent points come through to you. Either Jesus provided us enough information to determine whether or not this is the last generation, or He did not. If He did, it is pointless to argue something different. If He did not, it is pointless to even try to figure it out.

Either Jesus is correct, or people like Harold Camping are correct. My bet is with Jesus any day of the week. He is my authority. His Word is either truth or not. Who is *your* authority?

Fred DeRuvo, February 2011

1

THE OLIVET DISCOURSE

As we move into this year – 2011 – we will be noting some political changes that are taking place. These changes are moving us toward a time when the entire world will become as one. It will also move us to a point where one world ruler will rise up and take the lead.

I know, that sounds far-fetched and even gloom and doom. How could one person rise up to take over the entire world in the present day? For that to happen, obviously a number of things must occur to pave the way. Things like:

- A complete economic crash
- A severe food shortage
- Civil wars rising to an unprecedented level

Just these three things I've mentioned are on the verge of happening throughout the world. The European Union (EU) is close to collapsing, and by the way, America is not that far behind. Economically, with the way our current administration has been spending money that does not exist, it has severely lowered the value of the dollar, and with the Fed deciding to print 650 million dollars worth of currency with nothing backing it up, the situation simply worsens.

Not sure if you've noticed, but food prices have begun to skyrocket. My wife and I see this nearly every week when we go grocery shopping. It is not uncommon to see things that used to cost a dollar and a quarter rise to a dollar fifty, and then to their current price of a dollar ninety-three cents! Price increases have affected many things in the grocery store. Because of crops being wiped out by floods and foul weather, things can only get worse.

Gas prices continue to rise during a time when they normally go down in price (at this writing). This trickledown effect causes everything to rise. Then we have the Obama healthcare plan (as of this writing, on its way to the Supreme Court to determine its constitutionality) that is said will cost *trillions* of dollars to implement - money the government does not have. Where do you think it will come from? That is correct! Your taxes and mine will pay for it, so we will wind up with even less in our wallets as time goes by though President Obama promised to not raise taxes if he became president.

Scientists are predicting solar flares starting next year that could wipe out part, or all, of the world's electrical grid. If that happens, at the very least it would put us back into the Stone Age. At the very worst, it will extinguish most of – if not all of – life on the earth. If the solar flares simply affect pockets of the world, then those nations will be put back into the Stone Age and the rest of the world will need to come to their aid to get them back up to speed. Who knows how long that could take?

With the rise of terrorism we will likely see an increase in suicide bombers, and they will appear throughout the world. We may also see some major hits by terrorists, including within the United States.

Now, all of this sounds like doom and gloom, I agree. But it is this type of scenario that is very realistic in that it *could* occur in the next year or two, and would cause the world to want to have a leader who could *solve* problems.

Think of it. Increased terrorism puts the world on the brink of all out war. Beyond that, if the EU collapses and the United States has an even harder time paying its bills, it could generate a partial to total worldwide economic collapse. If that happens, the likelihood of Martial Law taking effect is very good. If that happens, the U.S. Constitution would be set aside. With the Constitution set aside, decisions will be made based most likely on a *global* economic structure. The existing leaders would want to come together to create some type of system that divides the world into manageable parts.

Are you aware that a secret organization called The Club of Rome has already done that? A number of years ago, a document was created by the individuals who belong to this elite club that parcels the entire world into *ten* sections, each governed by one person or a group of people. That this document exists is *fact*.

Interestingly enough, the book of Daniel speaks to the fact that the world will be divided into ten "nations" or areas, over which a king will reign. Daniel speaks of this in Daniel chapter 7, verses 23 and 24. *"A fourth kingdom on earth, Which shall be different from all other kingdoms, And shall devour the whole earth, Trample it and break it in pieces. The ten horns are ten kings Who shall arise from this kingdom.*

And another shall rise after them; He shall be different from the first ones, And shall subdue three kings."

Here, Daniel speaks of a fourth kingdom that devours the whole earth. This is yet to happen. There has never been a kingdom that devoured the entire earth. Even when phrases like this were used to describe kingdoms in the Bible that existed, the term meant the whole *known* earth.

This coming kingdom will cover the entire globe and from that – as it states in verse 24 – there will be *ten horns*, or as Daniel tells us, *ten kings*, who will rise up out of this approaching one-world kingdom. Interestingly enough, one individual will rise up from among those kings and begin to take control of *all* the kingdoms.

So where are we? Suffice it to say that we are solidly on our way. Nation after nation today is going bankrupt. The EU is on the verge of collapse and their currency the Euro with it.

The United States is steadily drowning in insurmountable debt, yet this administration continues to spend. They even have their eyes on *your* 401k retirement account! This is how bad things are getting.

A world economic collapse could easily usher in a new period on earth that eliminates borders between countries and creates new ones so that only ten sections exist, each controlled by one person, who will eventually answer to one other person.

This may sound unbelievable to some, but hiding your head in the sand or changing the channel on the TV will not solve the problem. There *is* a response to this and the response is to understand who Jesus is and why He came to this earth. He died for you and He died for me. He claimed to be God and did things only God could do. What are you going to say to that? That is the *only* question that matters.

The truth of the matter has a good deal to do with where this world is headed, and if you've taken the time to listen to shows on prophecy or read a book about it, one thing seems clear. It is apparent that this world is heading somewhere and it is ramping up to that point rather quickly.

The world just celebrated Christmas of 2010. It is likely that most people spent money that they did not have to buy gifts that they did not need. How much more in debt are you now than prior to Christmas of 2010?

For many, if not most, Christmas has become an event where we simply buy gifts and share the time with family and loved ones. Except for the people who regularly attend church, little thought is given to the actual reason behind the season.

What will Christmas of 2011 look like? Will the world even have one? I know that sounds defeatist; however, with the financial experts and prognosticators warning us about how close we are to economic collapse, it is a question that deserves an answer, and the answer may be more obvious than we think.

The weirdest part is that most people seem completely unaware of what is happening not only in our nation, but in our world. The coming events are here – on the horizon – and too many people cannot see them at all.

Far too many people who attend church go to church on Sunday and continue their normal lifestyle the other six days. Neither the church nor the Bible seems to have any real impact on people, even those who attend church.

Why is this? Is it because most churches today preach little to nothing from the Bible, but are content to simply talk about *social* injustice and other social problems that our world faces? It is as if many pastors today believe that the problems of the world can be solved without any involvement from God. *"No thanks God, we can handle it! That is all!"* In truth the gospel of Jesus Christ has been and continues to be replaced with a *social* gospel, a gospel that says, *"Look, all we need to do is help people improve their lives and all will be well."* Unfortunately, that does not deal with man's heart problem.

Yes, Christians need to be involved in feeding the hungry, visiting those in prison, doctoring the sick, and providing for the needy. However, none of this does what only the gospel of Jesus Christ does – none of those things provides eternal life! Yet too many churches preach that helping people is the meaning of being a Christian.

So we have tons of people who claim to be Christians running around this globe doing nothing except living life as if things will continue forever the way they are now, with ups and downs, but with all things equaling out in the end. Is that the way it is? Is that the way it is going to be?

The Bible speaks of a reality that I believe is thoroughly applicable to this generation of people, probably more than any other previous generation, and whether we like it or not, we need to deal with it.

I'll go out on a limb and state that I believe we are living in the last generation before the Lord returns. *"What?! Come on Dr. Fred, don't be a moron! Are you turning into one of the gloom and doom preachers who constantly talks about the end of the earth?"*

The truth is that I *believe* the Bible because I believe the One who wrote it. I believe it to be inerrant, practical, and fully applicable to our lives *today*. I do not believe the Bible contains error, nor do I believe that the Bible has contradictions. When people tell me that the Bible has contradictions, I ask them to point even one out to me. Most cannot do it because they are simply repeating what others have said. For the ones who *can* do it, the things they believe to be contradictions are not even close to being authentic contradictions.

All it takes is a bit of study about the culture of the Bible and it is amazing how the doors of understanding open up.

I believe the Bible to be infallibly written by God. I believe He chose to use roughly 40 human authors over a period of approximately 1,600 years to create a book that has no equal. The consistency found within the text of the Bible is unique and unparalleled. No other book including the Qur'an even comes close to the consistency, the uniqueness, the richness, and the truth of the Bible. Nothing.

Based on this then, yes, I believe we are moving to a point in time when Jesus will literally return to this earth. There are many ways to prove this from the Bible, but ultimately, it depends upon what a person thinks of the Bible, and what they are willing to learn from it.

First of all, Jesus Himself spoke of His own return. He said He was coming back, so to disregard that is to call Him a liar. Friends, Jesus is not a liar.

In Matthew 24, Mark 13, and Luke 21, we read of Jesus' teachings in what is one of His most famous sermons, second only to the Sermon on the Mount, found in Matthew 5-7.

These sections of Scripture – Matthew 24, Mark 13, and Luke 21 – are referred to as the Olivet Discourse because it was there on the Mount of Olives near Jerusalem that Jesus spoke these words to His disciples.

In the Olivet Discourse, Jesus explains what is going to take place toward the end, just prior to His return.

This is the fascinating thing about the Bible. The Bible is filled with prophetic utterances and prophecies, many of which have already come true, with some yet to be fulfilled. This is the most astounding part of the Bible because it is God telling the world, "*I am going to re-*

veal things to you ahead of time and when they come true, you will KNOW that I am God and that I am telling the truth."

There were more than 400 prophecies connected to Jesus alone, showing Him to be Messiah. Yes, that's *four hundred*, most of them written centuries before He appeared on this planet. While some modern day critics believe that the Bible was written backwards – in other words the events happened, and then someone created or redacted an existing document to make it appear prophetic – there is no evidence for this at all. In fact, people who try to put forth this type of rhetoric are people who end up looking extremely stupid because of their claims.

Let's take a look at the Olivet Discourse and see what, if anything, Jesus says to us about the time just before He returns. We can then determine if it's just a bunch of hogwash that television preachers have used to scare people into giving money, or if it is fact, based on the words of Jesus Himself.

Some believe there are contradictions or indiscernible words that Jesus spoke. Is that true? If so, it would make it impossible to comprehend anything about His return, and maybe we have misrepresented the whole issue. I don't believe it for a minute. Jesus spoke in parables, yes, but those parables always had *one* meaning. The meaning was not up for grabs. Jesus often spoke directly, without the use of parables, making His words even that much more clear.

Let's take a look and see how far we get during the remainder of our time together today.

Setting the Scene
Jesus has just had another head to head with the Pharisees in the previous chapter. For those who are not sure what "Pharisee" means, the Pharisees were a group of religious leaders that rose up during the time between the Old and New Testaments. They were an

extremely *legalistic* group, putting tradition above the actual Law of Moses as the guide for living. This of course made them even angrier at Jesus and more determined than ever to get rid of Him because of how He stood up to them and their error.

As Jesus passes by Herod's Temple, a few of His disciples marvel at the beauty of the Temple and its ornate design. This is where we pick up chapter twenty-four of Matthew.

Matthew 24:1-3
Jesus came out from the temple and was going away when His disciples came up to point out the temple buildings to Him.

And He said to them, "Do you not see all these things? Truly I say to you, not one stone here will be left upon another, which will not be torn down."

As He was sitting on the Mount of Olives, the disciples came to Him privately, saying, "Tell us, when will these things happen, and what will be the sign of Your coming, and of the end of the age?"

It is important to note here that after Jesus pointed out that the Temple would be completely destroyed with not one stone resting on another, the disciples understandably became very curious.

Notice they came to Him with a number of questions.

One, *when will these things happen?*

Two, *what will be the sign of your coming?*

Three, *what will be the sign of the end of the age?*

2

THREE QUESTIONS

We noted that in Matthew 23, Jesus had a head-to-head with the legalistic sect known as the Pharisees. They were constantly arguing with Him and always lost the debate. This caused their anger and resentment of Jesus to grow to a point where they simply wanted Him dead.

Please note that the disciples not only wanted to know *when* the Temple would be destroyed, but they also felt emboldened to ask

Him two other questions about His return and the end of the age. This is important to understand because it is only in seeing that the disciples wanted to know *more* than simply when Jerusalem and the Temple would be destroyed that we begin to comprehend the entire issue.

This clues us in to the fact that the disciples understood Jesus to be talking about *the* end, not simply the end of *their* generation, but the actual *end* of the *age*. This is clear because in Jewish vernacular and understanding, there are only two ages: this current age, and the age of the Messiah yet to come.

When Jesus came to this earth the first time, He was roundly rejected by the religious leaders of Israel when He offered Himself as Messiah. This He did when He rode into Jerusalem on the colt of a donkey, which we call the triumphal entry, and you can read about this in all four of the gospel accounts: Matthew 21:1-11, Mark 11:1-11, Luke 19:29-44, and John 12:12-19. In essence Jesus came to be the sacrificial Lamb for humanity. He was crucified during the time of the Jewish Passover.

You will likely recall that as Jesus rode into Jerusalem, the people placed palm branches and even their garments on the ground before Him and they cried out "*Hosanna!*" The religious leaders did not like this because they viewed this as blasphemous. They knew what was up, even though people argue about it today.

In fact, the religious leaders said to Jesus that He should command the people to stop saying "*Hosanna!*" which was a form of praise given to God *alone*. Jesus responded by telling them that if the crowd stopped, the very stones would cry out.

Both Matthew and John allude to the fact that this triumphal entry of Jesus was a direct fulfillment of **Zechariah 9:9**, which states:

"Rejoice greatly, O daughter of Zion; shout, O daughter of Jerusalem: behold, your king coming unto you; he is just, and having salvation; lowly, and riding upon a donkey, even upon a colt, the foal of a donkey."

The fact that, in spite of Jesus being received as royalty here, He is later rejected by the leaders of Israel tells us that there was some unfinished business. But even with that, Jesus came specifically to die for the sins of humanity and anyone and everyone who places their faith in His *finished* work on the cross receives salvation. It is so simple a cave man could do it, yet many refuse it because it *is* so simple! Salvation is something Jesus gained for humanity on the cross. Because of that, it is *nothing* we must or even *can* earn. It is a free gift.

By the time we arrive at Matthew 24, the triumphal entry has already occurred, and Jesus completely understands that His time on earth is coming to a close. He knows that the Jewish leaders will reject Him and turn Him over to Gentiles, who will execute Him.

Since Jesus completely understands that His execution is at hand, He endeavors to teach His disciples what they can expect not only in their lifetime, but when the actual end of the age arrives.

Understandably, the disciples were a bit confused. They thought Jesus came to usher in God's Kingdom and to overthrow Roman rule, setting the nation of Israel *free* from that tyranny. While He *did* come to do that, He also knew He would be rejected. That was also part of the plan, because He knew in being rejected He would be crucified, and in being crucified He would not only open the way for men and women to receive His salvation, but would also gain the title deed to earth, the very same earth that Satan had stolen from Adam and Eve through the fall.

This complex plan was only partially known to Satan. Satan concentrated on getting the people of Israel to reject Jesus and kill Him.

Satan assumed that once Jesus was dead, no one would be able to stop him from having full control over the earth. What Satan did not count on – because he could not see it – was that the salvation message culminated in the death, burial, and *resurrection* of Jesus Christ! Having accomplished salvation, Jesus literally held Satan up to ridicule and *legally* took back from him the title deed to earth.

This is the very same title deed that we read about in Revelation *chapter five*.

Getting back to **Matthew 24**, Jesus begins His discourse with a dire warning, and that warning still stands for us today. In fact, I believe that in light of what is occurring throughout the world today, this warning is particularly applicable to all people who are alive in what I believe is *the last generation*.

Matthew 24:4-5
And Jesus answered and said to them, "See to it that no one misleads you.

"For many will come in My name, saying, 'I am the Christ,' and will mislead many."

This is extremely important and cannot be underemphasized. In these two verses – *four* and *five* – Jesus specifically warns His disciples that as time progresses toward the end of the age, there will be more and more individuals who claim to be Messiah. Jesus' warning about not being misled is very clear.

"*See to it that no one misleads you*" is very strong language in the original Greek. It is similar to when your boss might come to you with a very urgent situation. After he explains the situation to you, he says, "*See to it that you get this done by the deadline.*" He's not asking you. He's telling you that this *must* be done, no ifs, ands, or buts.

This is what Jesus is saying. He is *not* saying, "*Hey folks, be aware that some people may try to mislead you telling you that they are the Christ, the Messiah.*" Jesus is saying in very clear and concise words that people *will* come for the specific purpose of leading people astray. DO NOT LET THAT HAPPEN TO YOU! It is very forceful.

What have we seen in this generation and the last few? We have seen a rise in people who are claiming to be Jesus Christ, or the Messiah. In the 70s, we had Sun Yung Moon and a few others. Today, we have many individuals claiming to be the Messiah, or Jesus. One such individual by the name of Apollo C. Quiboloy has an extremely large church in the Philippines. This person fully believes that he has been appointed the Son of God! He states it any number of times on his website, making no bones about it.

What is more troubling to me than the fact that Quiboloy is claiming to be Jesus is the fact that he has such a huge following of people! These individuals take what he says as truth, yet if what he says *is* truth, then the Bible cannot be true, because he is contradicting the Bible!

There are other individuals alive today who will tell you with a straight face that they are Jesus, the Messiah, or someone else of biblical importance. One such individual is Ronald Weiland, who firmly believes that he is one of the two witnesses spoken about in the book of Revelation, primarily in chapter *eleven*.

According to Revelation, these two witnesses will prophesy for 3 ½ years. Interestingly enough, Weiland will tell you that God has anointed him as one of these witnesses. The other witness? Why, it is his wife, of course. Together, these two people will allegedly prophesy to the earth for 42 months (as described in Revelation 11) until they are killed by the Antichrist.

Weiland also believes that all seven of the seals spoken of in Revelation have already occurred.[1] This is clearly not true, and the only way to arrive at that conclusion is to allegorize the Bible. When a person does this, the Bible can be made to say anything.

Imagine if you wrote a letter to a loved one. They receive your letter and after reading it, store it away. Years later, after that individual dies, another relative finds the letter along with others that you had written.

They read them and decide that the meaning found within the written words has nothing to do with your original meaning! They decide arbitrarily to place *their* meaning over your words, causing your letters to in fact say something else entirely.

A good deal of poetry is often allegorical. It can be understood several ways, and sometimes even the author leaves the meaning open-ended. Most literature, however, is *not* open-ended. Reading Moby Dick has a literal meaning to it. Even though the book is a work of fiction, it *still* has one meaning. The whale is not a figure of speech for something else. It is a whale!

Alice in Wonderland is a critically acclaimed, yet fairly weird, book. It seems to use imagination beyond the bounds of common sense. At times, it is difficult to really know what the author was attempting to tell us. Who knows; maybe he had gone mad like the Mad Hatter, and because of that the insanity prevalent within the Hatter found its way throughout the book.

My point is that when we approach the Bible (or any book of literature), we do so with the intent to take that book literally. By this, it is not meant literalistically, which does *not* take into consideration fig-

---

[1] For more on this, please read the author's forthcoming book, *End of the Ages*, a commentary for the layperson on the book of Revelation

ures of speeches, etc. Here is an example: *"I am so hungry, I could eat a horse!"*

If I said that, or you said that, it would be wrong to think that what was meant by that was that I was actually planning on eating a horse. It simply means I am very *hungry* and I have used figurative language to express that point.

Most people understand this and have little problem with it. However, many people who read the Bible arrive at figures of speech, metaphors, or parables and toss logic out the window! They assume that the meaning is buried deeply beneath the words. This is why Dan Brown's books are so compelling for many people, because they reinforce the belief that many have regarding the Bible; that it is a book of allegory, with the true meaning waiting to be uncovered.

In truth, understanding the Bible is not that difficult at all. In fact, it can be downright similar to the way we understand any book. When I read Scripture, I take it in its most plain, ordinary sense of meaning, until the text demands that another way should be used.

So when Jesus spoke in parables, I read the words and still ask myself, *"What exactly did Jesus MEAN in this parable or that one?"* A parable is like a story with a moral to it. The moral of the story provides us with the truth that the parable reveals.

We are not free to *take* meaning from the Bible that is not there, or *read* meaning *into* the Bible because it may make sense to us. We *must* always endeavor to understand the meaning of the Bible based on context, and that includes not simply the words surrounding something, but the culture in which those words were stated.

Since language changes so often, what means one thing to us today may have meant something completely different when Jesus said it. It is important for us to know what was originally meant. There are a number of these metaphors included in this Olivet Discourse that we will be discussing.

Right now, Jesus has issued the warning – *Imposters will come. They will try to brainwash you. Do NOT believe them!*

3

BIRTH PANGS

After cementing the principle about avoiding deception by false Messiahs, Jesus moves on to verse six of Matthew 24.

Matthew 24:6
You will be hearing of wars and rumors of wars. See that you are not frightened, for those things must take place, but that is not yet the end.

Do you notice that Jesus is saying that no matter how badly people *want* peace, it will not happen? We can sing or chant "Give Peace a

Chance," or "Imagine," until we run out of breath. In fact, the entire world can line up singing that song and it will make not one bit of difference! Jesus has clearly noted that wars and rumors of wars are going to be the norm until the end.

People get so upset about wars, and rightly so. The problem though is that as long as there are people in this world who are greedy and see themselves as demagogues, demigods, or dictators, the world will always have some element of war and skirmish occurring somewhere on the planet.

Jesus says that those things should *not* frighten us. Why? Because the end is not yet. Apparently, just before He returns, the world is going to become worse and worse. We will get to that soon.

Matthew 24:7
For nation will rise against nation, and kingdom against kingdom, and in various places there will be famines and earthquakes.

What we have just read is what is called an *idiom*. This is in fact a Jewish idiom used during the time of Christ that has a specific meaning. It has *one* meaning. It is not open for discussion, nor is it up for grabs. Prior to the Tribulation starting, Jesus pointed out in His Olivet Discourse (Matthew 24, Mark 13, and Luke 21) that when the world *begins* to experience certain things – and He listed them – we would know that this was the beginning of what He termed *birth pangs*. Birth pangs are just that, pains and cramping in the abdominal area that signals to the mother she is very close to giving birth.

At long last, the nearly ten months in which a human being needs to gestate are nearly over, and soon the husband and wife will be proud parents of a new and hopefully healthy baby.

Obviously, Jesus was likening the end to birth pangs because of the increasing problems that will face the world. These problems would start out fairly mildly, but end with a bang. They would build up to a crescendo, ending in His return to this earth.

This is exactly what is going to happen throughout the earth and in fact *is* happening now. Things will take place that will be very much like the birth pains that signal to the mother she is near to giving birth. The end of her pregnancy is very near.

The Olivet Discourse, which is recorded for us in Matthew 24, Mark 13, and Luke 21 all say the same thing *essentially*. There are a few differences so it is important to read all three versions to determine what is missing from one to the other. These are not contradictions or mistakes. They are simply the vantage point of the individual human author.

Dr. Arnold G. Fruchtenbaum points out nine birth pangs that we are to note in his book *Footsteps of the Messiah*. These are important events and signal things that are not to be missed. If we look carefully at the narratives, we note that the disciples asked Jesus three questions about the timing of the things that He had just finished discussing.

The reader will hopefully recall that as Jesus began His dialogue with the disciples about the End Times, he was referencing the Temple because the disciples had just marveled about how beautiful it looked. Jesus pointed out that there would come a time when not one stone will stand upon another (cf. Matthew 24:1).

The disciples then asked their questions, which were:

1. *When will these things be? (cf. Luke 21:20-24)*
2. *What will the sign of your coming be? (cf. Matthew 24:29-31)*
3. *What is the sign of the end of the age? (cf. Matthew 24:1-8)*

The entirety of the Olivet Discourse answers these questions (but note that question number one is only answered in the gospel of

Luke). Fruchtenbaum points out that Jewish people and especially rabbis thought in terms of *this age* and the *next age*, as previously mentioned. These are the two ages, the one we live in now and the one in the future when Messiah comes.

In essence then, the disciples were asking Jesus what *the* sign was that signaled the end of this age (the one in which we are now living), and the *beginning* of the next, or Messianic age.

In verses four through six of Matthew 24, Jesus points out two things to be aware of:

1. False messiahs
2. Wars and rumors of wars

Jesus immediately follows this up with, "*be not troubled: for all these things must come to pass, but the end is not yet*" in verse six. While false messiahs and local wars will happen, these do *not* signal the end of the age.

Birth Pang #1 – World Wars, Famines & Earthquakes

Jesus then goes onto point out what *does* signal the *start* of the end of the age. Two events or scenarios are important for us to grasp here.

1. *Nation shall rise against nation; kingdom against kingdom*
2. *Famines with earthquakes*

Dr. Arnold G. Fruchtenbaum points out that the phrase "*nation shall rise against nation and kingdom against kingdom*" is a Jewish idiom that refers to a *global* conflict, not merely a local one. In other words, the nations rising against nations and kingdoms against kingdoms are happening *at the same time*. This, he believes, clearly points to the First World War. Few, with the possible exception of Richard Abanes (see his book *End Times Vision*), would argue with that.

Interestingly enough, WWI gave rise to Zionism, a desire by Jews to return to their homeland. By the end of WWII, the establishment of the Jewish homeland via the resurrected nation of Israel was soon to be underway. This was due largely to Hitler's persecution of the Jews.

Unlike anything prior to it, WWI involved over 100 countries around the entire globe. No previous war involved that many nations or countries. All seven continents were involved as well. This was a truly global event, the first of its kind.

However, we not only note the First World War, but also need to determine whether famines and earthquakes were near that time as well since that is what Jesus says will occur. Some interesting statistics to note are:

- 1918-1919 (during war years)
    - 23 million people killed because of pestilence
- 1920 – Great Chinese Famine
- 1921 – Great Russian Famine

Beyond this, from Jesus' earthly walk to roughly 1,000 years afterwards, there were approximately five earthquakes recorded. Obviously, at least some of this is due to the fact that society lacked the scientific technology to record earthquake events. At the same time, one would think that earthquakes could still be felt and the larger ones would have been recorded or noted by someone.

From A.D. 63 to 1896, there were approximately 26 recorded earthquakes. It was not until 1905 that earthquakes began happening with much more regularity and with the loss of thousands of lives. The statistics break down like this:

- *14th Century   157 major earthquakes*
- *15th Century   174 major earthquakes*
- *16th Century   253 major earthquakes*

- 17th Century   278 major earthquakes
- 18th Century   640 major earthquakes
- 19th Century   2,119 major earthquakes
- 20th Century   over 900,000 earthquakes

The above information is according to the United States Geological Survey, National Earthquake Information Center, Earthquakes with 1,000 or more deaths from 1900 (May 12, 2000). Even though Jesus never said that earthquakes would *increase* during the time of nations and kingdoms rising against one another (He simply said they would happen), it is clear that this is exactly what happened.

In 2009 into 2010, earthquakes have gotten even more destructive, moving entire cities off their foundations and managing to compact the earth's crust. It should be obvious that since WWI, earthquakes along with famines are part of the historical landscape. The first birth pang then is World War I with accompanying earthquakes and famines, and this was initially fulfilled between the years 1914 to 1918. Remember, Jesus said that these were merely the *beginning of birth pangs*.

Birth Pang #2 – Israel Becomes a Nation
Zephaniah 2:1-2 speaks of something that Israel will do *before* the Tribulation. The text reads, *"Gather yourselves together, yea, gather together, O nation not desired; Before the decree bring forth, before the day pass as the chaff, before the fierce anger of the LORD come upon you, before the day of the LORD's anger come upon you."*

Many conservative scholars believe this refers to the beginnings of the re-established nation of Israel. Both Isaiah and Ezekiel refer to a worldwide re-gathering that would occur *prior* to the day of Jehovah (cf. Ezekiel 20:33-38; 36:22-24; Isaiah 11:11-12). Together these passages indicate that God Himself will bring about a return of His people to Israel, from which He will take His final remnant.

The phrase "*day of Jehovah*" is always used in the Old Testament to refer to the Tribulation period at the end of the age, just prior to Messiah's return. This is not referring to simply one "day," but a period of time that *includes* or *culminates* in the day of Jesus' return.

This re-gathering occurred in 1948 officially, when Israel again became a nation. See chart on the previous page.

Birth Pang #3 – Jerusalem No Longer Divided
It is interesting to note here that at the time Israel became a nation again, Israeli forces controlled:

- *West Jerusalem*
- *Newer Jewish section*
- *Old City of Jerusalem (the biblical city):*
    - *Fell into hands of Jordanian Legion*
    - *Later annexed into the Hashemite kingdom of Jordan*
    - *Jerusalem was divided city for 19 years*
    - *OT prophecies speak of Old City of Jerusalem falling under Jewish control*

On paper, when the *Six-Day War* ended, this gave Israel control of all of Jerusalem, which had remained divided for 19 years since the 1948 independence. During the Six-Day War, Moshe Dayan led his troops into the Old Jerusalem sector and after intense fighting gained control of the Western Wall *and* the Temple Mount.

Though the Temple Mount *remains* under Israeli sovereignty, shortly after the close of the Six-Day War in 1967 Israel allowed the control to remain in the hands of Islamic groups. This continues to be the source of problem for both Jews and Arabs since Jews are generally not allowed to pray on the Temple Mount, in spite of the fact that the area comes under the auspices of Israel's government.

So this third birth pang is a once again unified Old Jerusalem as indicated in Daniel 9:27, Matthew 24:15, and 2 Thessalonians 2:3-4. Not only is Jerusalem unified, but it remains under Israeli sovereignty.

Birth Pang #4 – Northern Invasion of Israel
Numerous scholars believe that prior to the beginning of the Tribulation an invasion of Israel will occur by a group of five nations, led by a leader referred to in Scripture as Gog. This title – not a name – may refer to the leader of this group from the north of Israel.

The main passage of Scripture referenced here is Ezekiel 38:1-39:16, which describes how God will actually bring the invasion about through the nations who have gathered together to overcome Israel. Not only will He bring the invasion about, but also will do the fighting *for* Israel.

> *"And the word of the LORD came unto me, saying, Son of man, set thy face against Gog, the land of Magog, the chief prince of Meshech and Tubal, and prophesy against him, And say, Thus saith the Lord GOD; Behold, I am against thee, O Gog, the chief prince of Meshech and Tubal: And* **I will turn thee back, and put hooks into thy jaws, and I will bring thee forth**, *and all thine army, horses and horsemen, all of them clothed with all sorts of armour, even a great company with bucklers and shields, all of them handling swords: Persia, Ethiopia, and Libya with them; all of them with shield and helmet: Gomer, and all his bands; the house of Togarmah of the north quarters, and all his bands: and many people with thee,"* (Ezekiel 38:1-6; emphasis added)

The interesting thing here is though God Himself brings this attempted invasion about, the players will still be held responsible for their actions, just as Judas Iscariot was for his. You have to appreciate the imagery when God says that He will "*put hooks into thy jaws, and I will bring thee forth."* Who can resist God? At the same time, all He will be doing is causing Gog to act on what is already in his heart.

As we continue in this narrative, note God's viewpoint recorded in verse fourteen through sixteen of Ezekiel thirty-eight.

> *"Therefore, son of man, prophesy and say unto Gog, Thus saith the Lord GOD; In that day when my people of Israel dwelleth safely, shalt thou not know it? And thou shalt come from thy place out of the north parts, thou, and many people with thee, all of them riding upon horses, a great company, and a mighty army: And thou shalt come up against my people of Israel, as a cloud to cover the land; it shall be in the latter days, and I will bring thee against my land, that the heathen may know me, when I shall be sanctified in thee, O Gog, before their eyes,"* (Ezek 38:14-16)

God is at the same time laying the blame squarely on Gog's shoulders, but also crediting Himself with making this happen. Why will God do this? For one simple reason: *to sanctify Himself before all the heathen.* In other words, God will *create* the problem that He will *solve* in order for the very world He created to know that He is God.

The remaining text of this chapter in Ezekiel provides us with an even heightened view of God's perspective.

> *"And it shall come to pass at the same time when Gog shall come against the land of Israel, saith the Lord GOD, that my fury shall come up in my face. For in my jealousy and in the fire of my wrath have I spoken, Surely in that day there shall be a great shaking in the land of Israel; So that the fishes of the sea, and the fowls of the heaven, and the beasts of the field, and all creeping things that creep upon the earth, and all the men that are upon the face of the earth, shall shake at my presence, and the mountains shall be thrown down, and the steep places shall fall, and*

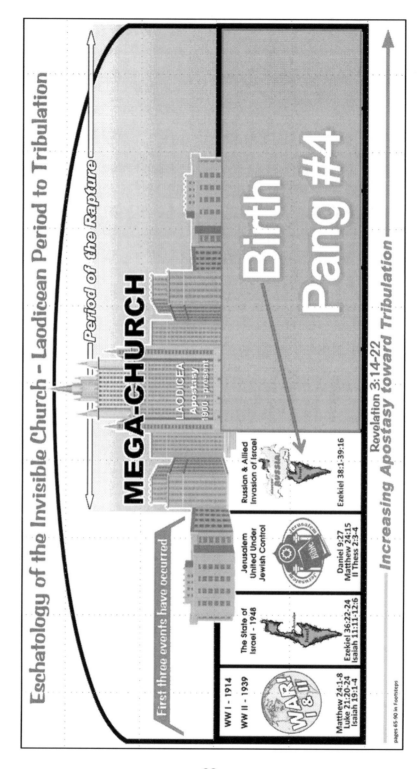

every wall shall fall to the ground. And I will call for a sword against him throughout all my mountains, saith the Lord GOD: every man's sword shall be against his brother. And I will plead against him with pestilence and with blood; and I will rain upon him, and upon his bands, and upon the many people that are with him, an overflowing rain, and great hailstones, fire, and brimstone. Thus will I magnify myself, and sanctify myself; and I will be known in the eyes of many nations, and they shall know that I am the LORD," (Ezek 38:18-23)

Can God be any clearer here in the text? Here is what He promises He will cause to happen when Gog leads the coming invasion:

- *A major earthquake throwing down the mountains and noticed by*
    - *The fish*
    - *The birds*
    - *The creatures of the earth*
    - *Humanity*
- *Nothing shall be left standing*
- *Soldiers will turn on each other*
- *Pestilence (disease) and blood*
- *God will join the fray by lobbing the following on the invaders*
    - *Hailstones*
    - *Rain*
    - *Fire*
    - *Brimstone*

Again, why does God do this? So that no one will misunderstand, Ezekiel tells us again that God does this to glorify *Himself*! Amen! This creates a time when the nations and the people of the earth will *know* that He is God! However, for how long will this last? Certainly, many within Israel will begin to come around to the fact that Jesus

Christ was and remains the true Messiah, but certainly not all of Israel will believe. God has just begun calling His remnant.

It reminds me of the few times (thankfully) when I knew my dad was going to be angry with me. I had blown it and was now waiting for the other shoe to fall. I became the politest kid around in an effort to show my dad that I had really changed and that I had all of a sudden grown past the ability to do something stupid again! It was not long, though, before the punishment came; then it was over, and within a few days, things returned to normal. I do *not* consider myself to have been a bad kid, but there were certainly times when I acted very stupidly and got what I deserved. Thankfully, my father loved me enough *to* discipline me.

This is likely the way it will be during the time just after this attempted invasion. God will prove that He and He alone deserves our praise and adoration. He will sanctify His Name because Israel certainly has not done it.

What people fail to realize is that Jerusalem is God's Holy City and the Land that He gave Israel is *His* Land. In fact, stop and consider how often people who become dictators treat parts of this world as if they own it. I do not recall God ever giving that dictator the title deed to earth, Israel, or Jerusalem.

Based on the Scriptural text, numerous Bible scholars believe that the following nations or groups are involved in this attempted invasion of Israel:

- *Russia*
- *Iran*
- *Ethiopia*
- *Somalia*
- *Germany*
- *Armenia*

Are the above the nations who will be after Israel? It could be, though some are not as sure. In either case, it looks as though the surrounding nations will be the perpetrators of this act of war and God will preempt it before it even gets off the ground.

Birth Pang #5 – One World Government
This birth pang is related to the world and its governmental process. In today's world, there are major economic upheavals throughout. America is reeling from debt, joblessness, and an unsure future, with little confidence in our leaders.

This is happening throughout the world and what will likely occur is a total devastation of world economies. This will prompt people to call for governments to do something - *anything* - that will cause people to regain confidence in their governments.

The only answer for this will be a one-world government. This one-world government will be touted as the only way to solve earth's problems. We will have become a global village, no longer separated by borders. The only reasonable solution to the problems our world faces is to have one government that rules over all of it.

This is outlined for us in Daniel 7:23-24, when the last Gentile kingdom – the 4th kingdom of Daniel 7 – will grow until it "devours" the world. Once the East-West axis of power derails, it will give way to a One World Government. In light of Ezekiel 38:1-39:16, the eastern balance of power will collapse with the fall of Northern forces (possibly Russia) and her Muslim allies in Israel and the destruction of the Northern area itself.

Birth Pang #6 – Ten Kingdom Stage
Once the one-world government is firmly in place, it will divide into ten districts, with a leader over each district. The entirety of the ten districts will fall under the rule of one leader.

Living in the Last Generation

Living in the Last Generation

43

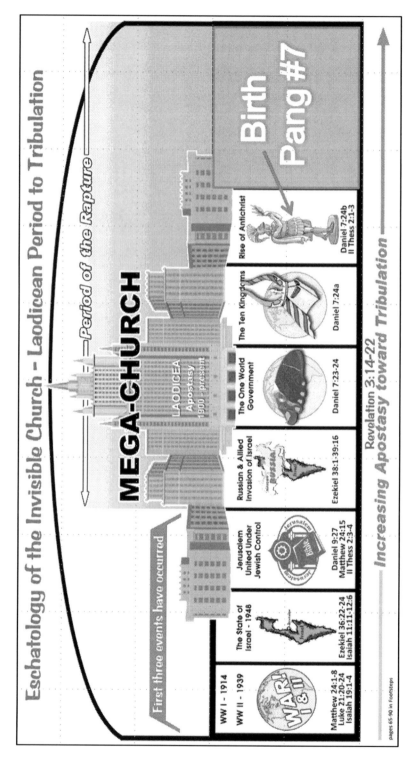

This ten-district unity will continue into the Tribulation period. It is from this ten-district system that the Antichrist will make his move to rise to the top of the heap.

Prior to the actual start of the Tribulation, the two things that must occur according to 2 Thessalonians 2:1-3 are:

- A great apostasy, or falling away
    - This does not mean that actual Christians will cease to be Christians. It means that those who have *professed* to be Christians will deliberately move away from the faith they once claimed to possess.
- The man of sin must be revealed
    - As stated earlier, the man of sin will reveal himself prior to the Tribulation as the savior of the world

We do not know just exactly *how* the Antichrist will be known because the Bible does not tell us. It is possible that a numerical value of his name could be applied (Hebrew naturally has a numerical system for each letter).

Birth Pang #7 – Rise of Antichrist

Ultimately, it is simply not known how the world will know him. His rise to power is a biblical *necessity* because the Tribulation cannot begin until Israel signs a 7-year agreement with him. This then is the seventh birth pang, the covenant with Israel for seven years.

When this occurs, Israel will believe she is safe from assault for at least the seven-year period that she has agreed upon with the Antichrist. The other nations that will agree to this will also give Israel a sense of security; however, it will be a false sense of security that is ultimately undermined by Antichrist himself.

As we will note, during the first half of the Tribulation Antichrist keeps a relatively low profile. He rides in on a white horse pretending to be a savior, but is actually the devil incarnate. He promises peace, but brings anything but peace.

Aside from God's judgments being poured out onto the earth during the first half of the Tribulation, Antichrist will be busy waiting for his moment of self-glorification when he enters the rebuilt Temple, sits down in the Holy of Holies, and declares himself god. He will demand to be worshiped and those who refuse will be hunted down and killed. This is when he will be ultimately unmasked to the Jewish people and they will run to the hills.

Birth Pang #8 – False Peace

Even though building up to the Tribulation there may *appear* to be a time of security, the events of the Tribulation will destroy that security. As we will see, the noticeable ramping up of intensity of events will be made clear.

The false sense of peace and security is the eighth birth pang.

Birth Pang #9 – Covenant Kicks off Tribulation

The actual covenant that Antichrist makes with Israel and other nations surrounding her is the ninth birth pang. This of course is where the Antichrist is revealed to the world, and we refer to Paul's words in 2 Thessalonians 2:1-3 already noted.

The problem of course is that some individuals are *assuming* that he is revealed for the first time when he actually defiles the Temple by declaring himself god and desecrating the altar within the Temple. This is when his true identity is revealed to the Jews, but the world has already recognized him as *the* world leader, the Savior of the world who has come to right all wrongs.

The idea that the Antichrist is *not* revealed to the world through his efforts to achieve peace with the covenant he brokers with Israel and surrounding nations is erroneous. It is at this point – birth pang #9 – when the Antichrist *reveals* himself to the world as its savior.

Living in the Last Generation

Living in the Last Generation

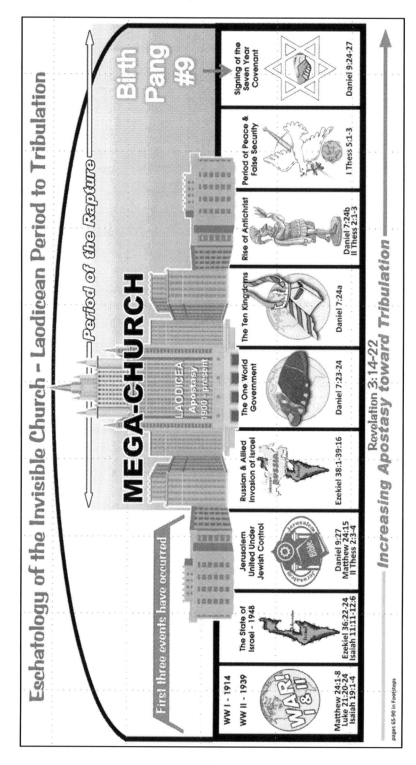

When he defiles the Temple, he will be revealing his authentic character – the devil incarnate – to the *Jewish people*. This will cause them to realize that they have been conned. They will then run to the hills, where God will offer his protection to them.

Because Antichrist is unable to spend his anger on the Jews, he will instead turn his terror on those who have rejected him as savior of the world.

The event of defiling the Temple occurs in the middle of the Tribulation and begins what Christ in the Olivet Discourse calls "great tribulation" (cf. Matthew 24). From this point onward, three and a half years remain of unbridled terror.

The Antichrist will release his own anger on God's people (along with all who refuse to receive him and his mark), while God will continue to pour out His wrath-filled judgments on the earth. It will be the most horrific time this earth and its citizens will have ever known.

It is clear that a number of these birth pangs have already occurred:

- *WWI with earthquakes, pestilence, and famines*
- *Israel becomes a state in 1948*
- *Jerusalem is united under the sovereignty of Israel*

The remaining birth pangs are still future, and it is possible that we may see the Invasion of the Northern Alliance soon. Daily in the news we read of the potential of Israel's preemptive attack on Iran in an effort to destroy Iran's nuclear capabilities.

If this preemptive strike occurs, it may well cause other countries to retaliate against Israel. If they retaliate, it may well be this Northern Alliance that does the retaliating on behalf of the nations in the Middle East.

If the Northern Alliance takes place, God has promised to intervene, and it appears according to Scripture that if He does so He will personally defend Israel without Israel's armies having to raise a finger. He does this for the sake of His Name and for His own glory. Before we get into Revelation proper, we will deal briefly with the power that Satan has and the limits God has placed on him.

4

AFTER THE BIRTH PANGS

We have just gone through the Birth Pangs that lead up to the end of the age. These birth pangs not only occur prior to the start of what Jesus will refer to as the Tribulation, but will carry on into the Tribulation period.

Matthew 24:9
Then they will deliver you to tribulation, and will kill you, and you will be hated by all nations because of My name.

This is a sad commentary on life in the end times. Authentic believers in Jesus will be subjected to all types of terrible situations and injustices. In fact, the world will come to a point of hating anyone who claims to be a Christian. Of course, this will separate the professing Christians from authentic Christians. Who will want to be a Christian if they will have to deal with hatred from the world on a constant basis? People who are not true Christians will simply fall away, and the apostle Paul discusses this in 2 Thessalonians when he speaks of what he terms the great falling away, or the apostasy (cf. 2 Thessalonians 2:1-3). Paul also makes this same point in his letter to Timothy when he says, "*Now the Spirit speaketh expressly, that in the latter times some shall depart from the faith, giving heed to seducing spirits, and doctrines of devils*" (cf. 1 Timothy 4:1).

What we are seeing today is this taking place in society. What has been termed the Emergent Church began a number of years ago. It presented itself through people such as Brian McLaren, Rick Warren, and numerous others as enlightenment for Christians. It boasted of a higher calling, a higher purpose - but ultimately, that purpose is no different than many things that have come before it; it simply has another name.

The Emergent Church is the same old lie of the enemy in different clothing. This lie says that many roads lead to God, not only through Jesus. Not only do many roads lead to God, but maybe Jesus is not even God for everyone. Listening to or reading works by people like McLaren or Tony Campolo sheds light on the real meaning of the Emergent Church, and it is anything but authentic Christianity. Yet that is what it masquerades as to a world that knows no better.

In this day and age, the authentic Christian is coming under fire from a variety of sources, including the Emergent Church. People from the Emergent Church and the New Age Movement have something in common. They both see orthodox or authentic Christians as the *problem*, not the solution. Because authentic Christians are seen as the problem, something must be done to either shut them down or eliminate them altogether.

This is why Jesus is saying authentic Christians will be delivered *to* tribulation and even death. This will not be a local phenomenon, but one that reaches all ends of the world. This is happening today throughout the globe.

Persecution of authentic Christians is becoming more and more prevalent. Many countries throughout the world allow and even encourage persecution of Christians. India, China, Russia, and numerous other countries have terrible track records where human rights are concerned. It is common for Christians to be accused, tossed into jail without a trial, or even be formally charged. Christians have their homes taken right out from underneath them. Churches are destroyed. There is little to no recourse for the actions of the state as it steamrolls over Christians.

You would also think that in a day and age such as we live in, martyrdom would be virtually a thing of the past, except in those third world nations where barbarism is the law. Yet, in many nations that compete globally in the world of technology, Christians are being murdered at an unprecedented rate. There are a number of organizations that monitor this trend, and the numbers are not pretty.

According to one site, from 2008 to 2009, 176,000 Christians were martyred throughout the world. [2] The site went on to cite a report of *"North Korea, which reportedly uses Christians as guinea pigs to test chemical and biological weapons, as the world's worst persecutor of Christians."*[3] More and more Muslim countries are being added to the Open Doors "watch" list as persecutors of Christians. *"Open Doors estimates there are 100 million Christians worldwide who suffer interrogation, arrest and even death for their faith, with millions more facing discrimination and alienation."*[4]

---

[2] http://www.wnd.com/?pageId=143493
[3] Ibid
[4] Ibid

As this is being written, the Voice of the Martyrs Website lists a number of recent situations involving Christians and the persecution they suffer. *"On Jan. 3, a judge told Shoaib Assadullah that if he did not renounce Christ within one week he would face up to 20 years in prison or even be sentenced to death. Shoaib was arrested on Oct. 21, 2010, when he gave a man a Bible in Mazar-e-Sharif, the fourth largest city in Afghanistan. The man reported the incident to authorities, and Shoaib was arrested. He has been imprisoned in northern Afghanistan since his arrest."*[5]

In another instance: *"A 17-year-old girl who converted to Christianity from Islam was shot to death recently in an apparent "honor killing" in Somalia, according to Compass Direct News. Nurta Mohamed Farah, who had fled her village to live with relatives after her parents tortured her for leaving Islam, died on Nov. 25, according to the Compass Direct report."*[6]

There are many more news stories like these. *"On Nov. 22, three more believers were killed in Mosul, Iraq, according to the Assyrian International News Agency and Cable News Network. In this latest attack on the country's Christian community, assailants entered a shop owned by two Christian brothers, Saad Hanna and Waad Hanna, and shot them. Waad died at the scene, and Saad died from his injuries a few hours later. In a separate incident later in the day, police found an elderly Christian woman strangled in her Mosul home."*[7]

What we are seeing is an increase in persecution throughout the world against Christians. Because Christians do not fight back when on the receiving end of persecution, people know that they will receive little to no resistance. This makes Christians a very easy mark.

---

[5] http://www.persecution.com/public/newsroom.aspx?story_ID=MzI5
[6] Ibid
[7] http://www.persecution.com/public/newsroom.aspx?story_ID=MzIx

It is also a biblical fact that Christians should not resist during times of persecution.

It seems clear that the words of Jesus in verse nine of Matthew 24 have started to come true and we can expect a growing hatred from the world toward authentic Christians. Remember, those individuals who profess to be Christians, but are not authentic Christians, will find it easy to give up the ship when the going gets tough.

This is exactly His point in Matthew 24:10, which states, *"At that time many will fall away and will betray one another and hate one another."*

These are the individuals who attend church, may read their Bibles, and even pray or do other things that make them appear as Christians. They themselves may believe that they are in fact actual Christians, but one thing is missing: *there has been no real spiritual transaction* that Jesus speaks about in the gospel of John, chapter three. Without that spiritual transaction – new birth, birth from above – the authenticity is missing from the life of the person. They are Christians in name only. Because of that, walking away from Christianity will be fairly easy for them when the pressure ramps up because ultimately, they will want to save their own life. In doing so, they will wind up losing it...forever.

During the time leading up to and including the Tribulation, in an effort to protect their own lives many non-believers and professing Christians will eagerly point the finger at people they know to be true Christians. These individuals will be seen as standing against Christianity and Christians and their lives will be spared. They will not come under persecution because they will be directing the world's ire toward authentic believers, saving themselves from that same persecution.

Please understand that the world hates authentic Christians because of Jesus. Why is that? It is because the world hated Jesus when He lived here. This world is fallen, controlled by evil forces. When this same Jesus – through the Holy Spirit – lives within the authentic believer, it makes sense that the same hatred that existed when He walked this earth and was directed toward Him will be directed toward His authentic believers. As time progresses, a growing number of authentic Christians will wind up dying because of their belief in Jesus as Savior and Lord.

This results in a number of things that Jesus points out in verses 11 – 14. Here Jesus states, *"Many false prophets will arise and will mislead many. Because lawlessness is increased, most people's love will grow cold. But the one who endures to the end, he will be saved. This gospel of the kingdom shall be preached in the whole world as a testimony to all the nations, and then the end will come."*

Please note again that Jesus mentions *false prophets*. These false prophets will rise up with a message that tickles the ears of many people. It will likely be a variation of the New Age message that we are all gods. We are all divine within and we merely need to access that divinity. Once we do that, nothing will hold us back from doing whatever we want to do.

In many ways, this New Age message has been around since the beginning. We read of it in the Garden of Eden (Genesis 2) when Satan used the serpent to tempt Eve. We also read of it in Genesis 11 when Nimrod brought all the people living in the world at that time together to create a tower. Since the entire world at that time spoke in one language, there was no reason for people to separate into other areas of the world, so they remained together.

When Nimrod rose up, he began to unite people so that they literally had one voice. Together they all moved to the east on the large plain of Shinar. There is where he rallied the people to build a tower that would reach the heavens.

It is interesting to note here that even God said, "*Behold, the people is one, and they have all one language; and this they begin to do: and now nothing will be restrained from them, which they have imagined to do. Go to, let us go down, and there confound their language, that they may not understand one another's speech. So the LORD scattered them abroad from thence upon the face of all the earth: and they left off to build the city*" (Genesis 11:6-8).

Do you get the picture? Here God forcibly separated them by confounding their languages. This caused the people to move off into separate groups according to the speech that they recognized in other individuals.

Since the beginning, then, our mortal enemy Satan has been attempting to create a one-world society from all the various cultures throughout the world. Way back during Nimrod's time, there was only one language, therefore one culture. It was fairly easy for him to move the people to have one voice and one purpose. God threw a monkey wrench into it and essentially took the power out of Satan's attempt to unify everyone under heaven against God.

However, this is what he has continued to work at creating *again* since that time. Now, in 2011, nearly the entire world speaks one language – English. Even in third world countries we hear leaders and dignitaries of those countries speaking English.

The New Age Movement has been attempting to teach people that we are all "one," that we are all connected. They have done this by presenting the lie that we are gods. This is the exact same lie that Satan told to Eve through the serpent in the Garden of Eden

Nothing has really changed in life. Things continue along the same lines as they always have been. With each new generation of people, Satan has had a bit more success uniting them each time, and he has been uniting them against God. The common enemy is perceived to be *authentic* Christians. Without an enemy, the world would have no real reason to unite. With an enemy, the world has a real reason to unite. In doing so, they are uniting *against* God (by being against His children), and uniting *with* Satan, though they are unaware in most cases that this is what they are doing.

Notice also that Jesus says during this time that *lawlessness will increase* and *the love of most will grow cold* (cf. Matthew 24:12). Take some time to watch some of the better documentaries that have been produced on gangs and the growing violence in the world and what you will see will startle you. One documentary from National Geographic highlights one particular gang that had its humble beginnings in Los Angeles. Now, in 2011, it boasts over 10,000 members *across* the United States and over 150,000 members throughout the *world*. Authorities and law enforcement officials are most concerned about this particular gang because it has literally grown like a virus, and the violence associated with the gang itself surpasses other gangs by leaps and bounds.

With this type of violence in the cities (and even in the rural areas), as well as the constant threat of terrorism from al-Qaeda and other terrorist groups both within and without the United States, people are starting to close down emotionally. No longer are they interested in loving their neighbors. Their main concern is for their own safety. This obviously causes people to become more self-centered, and it becomes easier for these people to ignore concerns of others if it means that they might be caught in the crossfire of either gang or terrorist activity.

Jesus also points out that those who hang on until the end will be saved. This is often misunderstood by many. This is a warning that many take to mean an authentic Christian *can* lose their salvation. If we compare this to other areas of Scripture, we quickly realize (or should) that salvation is secure and eternal. This creates an apparent contradiction, but not a real contradiction.

When we receive the Holy Spirit, He seals us unto the day of redemption (cf. Ephesians 4:30). Romans 8 tells us that we are no longer condemned in Christ (cf. v. 1). The last part of that phrase, *"who walk not after the flesh, but after the Spirit,"* is not even in the first verse in a number of good manuscripts. Please note the exact same phrase is also used at the end of verse 4. It makes much more sense to have it there because it is presenting it as a *fact* of our life as Christians. In verse 1, it gives the appearance that the oneness is on us. This is *not* the case.

Some people also go so far as to suggest that even though Romans 8 ends with the promise that nothing can separate us from God's love (cf. vv. 38-39), they turn this around to say that *we* can make the decision to walk away from Jesus. This is absurd. As an example, Jesus spoke of a situation in which a person entering another's home would have to overcome the strong man (home owner).

Specifically, He says, *"Or else how can one enter into a strong man's house, and spoil his goods, except he first bind the strong man? and then he will spoil his house"* (cf. Matthew 12:29). Jesus had just been accused of casting out demons by the power of Satan. He replied that in essence, He is the stronger Man who owns the house. In that case, how would it be possible for a weaker man (Satan) to enter into that house and spoil it? It's a rhetorical question. See also Mark 3:27.

Yet we have people who believe we are stronger than God, that somehow our own free will is such that if we truly decide to walk away from Him, He will do nothing about it. This is because they do not understand the essence of our relationship with Jesus.

First of all, we have been *bought* with a price (cf. 1 Corinthians 6:20; 7:23). This price was Jesus' shed blood as He died a horrifically painful death on Calvary's cross. Do you understand that a person who is *bought* is no longer their own?

If we exercise faith in the work of Jesus Christ enough to see the truth and embrace that truth, we become new creatures and the Holy Spirit comes to indwell us and seal us, as has been mentioned. This seal represents *ownership*. From that moment onward, Jesus owns us. We are His slaves and He will spend the remainder of our earthly lives teaching us His ways and forming us into His character. He is the Author and Finisher of our faith (cf. Hebrews 12:2).

Since Jesus owns us, proof of which is the seal that the Holy Spirit places on us, He has a right to do with us as He will. It does not matter what we want. The Holy Spirit's job is to mold us into Jesus' image. At times, He may have to chastise us. At other times, He blesses us with a greater awareness of His presence through the truth of His Word.

Once we receive the salvation that Jesus has made available, there is never a time when our free will (such as it is) could ever overpower the stronger Man, Jesus. That is insane to think or believe that. It denigrates the power of God. It dishonors Him for thinking that His hands are tied when it comes to those whom He owns.

We are His sheep and we are the sheep in His pasture. He will no more stand aside to watch a wayward sheep head off out of the sheepfold into danger than He would allow us to do that. He *may* be inclined to give us some room to start hanging ourselves in order to show us that we are not as powerful as we think we are, but He will not stand by while we choose to use our puny free will to walk away from Him.

The only people that can walk away from Christianity are *professing* Christians. These are people who have some idea of the truth of Christianity. They have begun to understand it and aligned themselves with a church. They may even be involved in that church, but they have never received salvation, in spite of the fact that they may believe they have done so. These are the people who walk away from Christianity. Authentic Christians can never do this, in spite of what many believe.

Note that Jesus says the gospel will be preached throughout the entire world, and then the end will come. Now that is interesting, if we are to consider the fact that the love of the average person will grow cold, deception will be at an all-time high from false messiahs, and there will be unparalleled persecution of authentic Christians. What it says to me is that in spite of all of these things, authentic Christians will continue to preach Jesus and Him crucified. We will continue to preach to our neighbors, our co-workers, and strangers, by word and deed.

The gospel of the Kingdom will go out, and because of it the Lord will work in people's hearts to receive the only salvation that truly exists. People will continue to be saved, in spite of the terribly lawless and unloving attitudes that will exist during the end times.

This is an amazing awareness: that Jesus will work through His own children to present the gospel to a dying world in the midst of persecution, hatred, and strife. People will be saved and Christians will be the ones who are privileged to bring this message of hope to a dying world!

In essence then, God will be glorified.

IT'S AN ABOMINATION!

Jesus has just finished telling His disciples that the gospel will continue to go out to those living in this world and when it has gone *throughout* the entire world, the end will come. Now, immediately after saying that, He backtracks a bit to highlight a few more things that will take place in the world prior to His return.

What is fascinating here is that Jesus gives us plenty of notice. He warns us of these things ahead of time in order to give us a heads up. He does this for our benefit, not to scare us. He outlines the events so that when they occur, we will be reminded that He has already told us that certain things will happen.

This next event that Jesus shines the light of understanding on is extremely important and not to be missed.

Matthew 24:15
When ye therefore shall see the abomination of desolation, spoken of by Daniel the prophet, stand in the holy place, (whoso readeth, let him understand:)...

This is an event that every Jew alive during Jesus' day would have known of because it impacted Jewish history and culture and would never be forgotten. To understand what Jesus is talking about here, we must travel back in time to roughly 168 B.C. when Antiochus Epiphanes lived and ruled.

This is the interesting thing about the Bible, and it needs to be considered when studied. The Bible was not written in a vacuum. It was written within the context of past history. Even when prophetic passages speak about things future, it was still written within the context of history, and that history and culture must be taken into account.

"Antiochus IV Epiphanes (... born c. 215 BC; died 163 BC) ruled the Seleucid Empire from 175 BC until his death in 163 BC. He was a son of King Antiochus III the Great and the brother of Seleucus IV Philopator. His original name was Mithridates; he assumed the name Antiochus after he assumed the throne."[8]

Epiphanes was not the greatest ruler, as history shows. Certain of his defeats led to problems with the Jews. On one such occasion, while in Egypt, apparently a rumor of his death caused the deposed High Priest (who had been replaced by Menelaus, an appointment of Epiphanes) to gather troops in an attempt to retake what was lost.

---

[8] http://en.wikipedia.org/wiki/Antiochus_IV_Epiphanes

Upon hearing of this, Epiphanes became enraged and went to Jerusalem in order to set things straight. He sacked Jerusalem, again returning Menelaus to the position of High Priest, and in an attempt to solidify his power over the Jews he outlawed the Jewish Temple practices, insisting instead that the Greek god Zeus was to be worshipped. Moreover, he ordered unlawful items to be brought into the Temple, and in doing so wound up desecrating it.

It is also said that Epiphanes slaughtered a pig on the altar inside the Jewish Temple and sprinkled the pig's blood around the inside of the Holy of Holies. This act, along with the setting up of Zeus' statue, became known as the "abomination of desolation" or the "abomination that desolates."

This was also referred to in the book of Daniel, from the Old Testament. In Daniel 9:24-27 we read the following:

"24Seventy weeks are determined upon thy people and upon thy holy city, to finish the transgression, and to make an end of sins, and to make reconciliation for iniquity, and to bring in everlasting righteousness, and to seal up the vision and prophecy, and to anoint the most Holy.

"25Know therefore and understand, that from the going forth of the commandment to restore and to build Jerusalem unto the Messiah the Prince shall be seven weeks, and threescore and two weeks: the street shall be built again, and the wall, even in troublous times.

"26And after threescore and two weeks shall Messiah be cut off, but not for himself: and the people of the prince that shall come shall destroy the city and the sanctuary; and the end thereof shall be with a flood, and unto the end of the war desolations are determined.

"27And he shall confirm the covenant with many for one week: and in the midst of the week he shall cause the sacrifice and the oblation to cease, and for the overspreading of abominations he shall make it deso-

late, even until the consummation, and that determined shall be poured upon the desolate."

This is the only place in the entire Bible that speaks of the 70 weeks,[9] and it describes the times in which Gentile nations will oversee parts of Israel and Jerusalem.

The abomination is referred to in verse 27. Note that the entire verse refers to someone who confirms a covenant with "many" for one week. Without going into a great amount of detail, the word that has been translated "weeks" should have been translated *years*. The reason it is translated "weeks" is due simply to the context of the entire chapter. At the beginning of the chapter, the angel Gabriel presents Daniel with a bit of a play on words.

Daniel had been reading the book of Jeremiah and realized after much study and prayer that the Jewish captivity in Babylon was coming to a close, because according to Jeremiah, the 70 *years* was nearly up.

As Daniel seeks the Lord, Gabriel the angel is sent to him and essentially says, "*No Daniel, it's not 70 weeks (years), but 70 sevens of weeks (years).*" The word "weeks" is similar to using the word "dozen." While it is a specific number meaning twelve, it does not tell us what the dozen represents. In other words, if someone asks someone else to go to the store and purchase a dozen, the natural question would be, "a dozen what?"

The same thing applies here. The only reason we know that "weeks" ultimately equals "years" is because of the context. In essence then, in verse 27, when it states that "he shall confirm the covenant with many for one week," it really means "he shall confirm the covenant

---

[9] For more information on the 70 Weeks, please see the author's book *Between Weeks*.

with many for one *seven*, which ultimately means *one set of seven years*. This is an extremely brief explanation of the meaning.

Note the part of verse 27 that speaks of the "overspreading of abominations," and just prior to that, the text reads: "in the midst of the week (seven years, or 3 ½ years into this seven year period), he will cause the sacrifice and the oblation to cease." This is caused by the person in the passage (he who confirms the covenant) in order to do something that desecrates the Temple during the final seven years of human history just prior to the physical return of Jesus.

Going back to Jesus' words in Matthew 24, Jesus says, "*When ye therefore shall see the abomination of desolation, spoken of by Daniel the prophet, stand in the holy place, (whoso readeth, let him understand:)...*"

This is important for two reasons. Jesus is deliberately pointing the reader *back to* the book of Daniel. He is also stating clearly that the event of which He is speaking had not occurred yet, so it was still future from His perspective. By the way, the words "whoso readeth, let him understand" was included by Matthew as the human author of this gospel. That is not what Jesus stated, but Matthew added it as a reminder to those who would be reading this gospel account later on. Notice that he assumes that the readers will understand what he is talking about, and simply reminding them this way is seen as good enough.

The passage in Daniel speaks of an event that will not occur until during the final seven years of human history, and then Jesus will return to the earth. This is the event that Jesus is speaking of and He mentions it as a sign for those Jews who will be living at the time of this event. Jesus is painting broad strokes of His brush here because He rapidly moves from His present day to the days that are far beyond the reach of those who were alive at that time. It is important to note that Jesus, knowing that Matthew, Mark, and Luke would write their accounts, wanted it to be included in those gospels, even though the people who actually heard Jesus make these statements would *not* be alive at the time.

A careful reading of this text is needed to determine what was specific for Jesus' time and what was specific for things *after* Jesus' time. I personally believe we are fast approaching that time when the final seven years of human history will begin. It is clear from Daniel 9:27 that this seven years (or week) will start as soon as the "he" mentioned in that passage confirms a covenant with the many. The "many" here can be none other than the Jewish people, and specifically the leaders of Israel, who have authority to sign covenants on behalf of the citizens of Israel.

This part of the Matthew text is incredibly important because as we have seen, it ties in directly with the text in Daniel, and Daniel is the only passage in Scripture that discusses the 70 weeks. Jesus is stating that the desecration of the Temple by Antiochus Epiphanes was a precursor to another similar event that would occur at the end of the age, during the final seven years.

Jesus is stating that at that time, another individual would waltz into the Temple and desecrate it, just as Epiphanes had done in 168 B.C. Can we look to any other portion of Scripture to support this? Yes, Paul refers to this very same event of the future in which this man of the future will desecrate the Temple, and we have already touched on it.

In 2 Thessalonians 2:3-4 we read, "*Let no man deceive you by any means: for that day shall not come, except there come a falling away first, and that man of sin be revealed, the son of perdition; Who opposeth and exalteth himself above all that is called God, or that is worshipped; so that he as God sitteth in the temple of God, shewing himself that he is God.*"

Paul outlines the order of events before the big event can occur, something he calls the day of the Lord. Paul states that a falling away must occur. This includes the apostasy we have discussed already. Once the apostasy occurs, the individual he refers to as the "man of sin" will need to be revealed. Paul goes on to also call him the "son of perdition" (or of hell) and then extends the readers' understanding by describing additional things this man of sin will be known for doing.

Notice that Paul talks about how this man will oppose God. Paul also tells us that this man will exalt himself above everything that is called God. In other words, this coming man of sin will do everything possible to oppose God's order, will, and purposes, even doing his level best to raise himself *above* God. If you are at all familiar with Scripture, this should take you back to the fall of Lucifer, who became Satan. We read about him in Isaiah 14 and Ezekiel 28. Here we see *why* Satan fell, and he fell because of his plans.

Lucifer saw himself as beautiful and extremely wise. He eventually saw himself as someone who had been self-made. This led his ego to believe that he could actually attain a higher status than God Himself. Of course, this is not what occurred, but Satan has been retrying ever since and God has allowed it - but He has allowed it for His own purposes.

In the final seven years of human history, this man of sin, known as the Antichrist in the writings of the apostle John (both in his small epistles and also in the book of Revelation), will do everything he can to not only strive against God, but supersede Him. This is what Paul is saying here, that this man of sin will not only oppose God, but will do everything possible to raise himself above God, something he will ultimately not be able to do. He will certainly give it his best shot though, and the power that moves him will be the power of Satan (thus Paul's reference to the "son of perdition," or of hell).

Continuing to read Paul's words, we see that this man of sin does something specific that will wind up desecrating the Temple. As I have stated previously, passages such as this one give credence to the idea that at least part of the Jewish Temple will need to be rebuilt in order for this to occur. We can see that this coming man of sin will actually sit in the very Temple of God in an attempt to declare that he *is* God, and he will demand to be worshipped.

This very act will alert the Jews during that time that they have been deceived, and they will run for the hills, as Jesus instructs in the next few verses.

Some believe that this act will *reveal* this man of sin to the world and this is what Paul is talking about when he states that the man of sin will be revealed. This author is of the opinion that there will be Christians living during this time as well. This man of sin will be revealed to Christians as soon as he signs the covenant with the leaders of Israel, and that is the event that begins the final seven years.

What Antiochus Epiphanes did in 168 B.C. desecrated the Temple of the Jews then, and what the coming man of sin will do in the middle of the future final seven years will do the same thing. There is one difference. This final man of sin will be thoroughly empowered by Satan. In fact, there is a good chance he will be either the incarnation of Satan in human form, or he will be so completely overtaken and controlled by Satan that there will be very little difference between the two.

One more point to mention here. In A.D. 70, Jerusalem and the existing Temple were sacked by Roman troops. Not one stone was left on top of another during that event. Every stone was carted away by Roman soldiers and the gold that had overlaid many of these stones was melted away from the stones.

It is worthwhile to note, though, that the Temple was not desecrated by anyone during this event. No Roman leader or soldier went into the Temple and desecrated it by setting himself up as a god to be worshipped. We know this because the priests themselves started the fire that destroyed the Temple because they did not want the Temple to be desecrated by the Roman army, nor did they want aspects of the Temple to be carted away and used in what they would have considered to be abominable worship of pagan gods.

When the man of sin arrives on this planet, he enters into a covenant with the leaders of Israel that begins the seven-year period that commentators refer to as the Tribulation period. In the middle of this "week," or final seven years, the man of sin (or Antichrist) will deliberately waltz into the Temple and set himself up as god, insisting that all people worship him. This is the future event that Jesus is referring to here, and the A.D. 70 sacking of Jerusalem by Rome does not count. While it fulfills part of what Jesus stated would happen, it does not fit the rest of the prophecy.

We must wait for the time of the final seven-year period to occur in order for the last aspects of this prophecy to be fulfilled.

6

RUN AWAY! FLEE!

Matthew 24:16-20
Then let them which be in Judaea flee into the mountains: Let him which is on the housetop not come down to take anything out of his house: Neither let him which is in the field return back to take his clothes.

And woe unto them that are with child, and to them that give suck in those days! But pray ye that your flight be not in the winter, neither on the sabbath day.

Jesus makes no bones about it here. When the Jews see the Abomination of Desolation (that we discussed in chapter five), they should *flee*! They should waste no time in getting out of there because if they dawdle, they will likely lose their lives.

Jesus says that it will be bad for nursing mothers. Why? Simply because it will slow them down. He also tells them to pray that it will not happen on the Sabbath. Why? Because they will not be able to run away.

When the Six-Day War of 1967 occurred, Israel was attacked on the Sabbath Day, which meant that, to their way of thinking, they could not lift a finger to help themselves! They lost a good many people that day and it took two weeks before they were able to regain what they lost against their enemies.

By the way, the Six-Day War was when Israel was attacked by other nations out of the blue. Initially, Israel lost big, but not only managed over time to regain what was lost, but also managed to gain land that Israel did not have prior to that war. It was during that war when Israel gained control of all of Jerusalem and the Temple Mount.

Yet, in spite of the fact that Israel was attacked and won new areas fair and square, these same nations have been loudly protesting since then. They have been demanding that Israel return the land that was "stolen" during the Six-Day War. Unfortunately, Israel has acquiesced over the years and given back property that was gained through war.

In the future, when Antichrist desecrates the rebuilt Temple, the Jews will realize that they have been bamboozled and will need to literally run for their lives. This will not be a time of celebration but of panic, because the Antichrist, realizing that the Jews will not bow down to him, wants nothing more than to eradicate all living Jews. This is a tragic situation, but it is made possible because the leaders of Israel trust the Antichrist enough to believe that his motives are altruistic.

Matthew 24:21-25
For then shall be great tribulation, such as was not since the beginning of the world to this time, no, nor ever shall be.

And except those days should be shortened, there should no flesh be saved: but for the elect's sake those days shall be shortened.

Then if any man shall say unto you, Lo, here is Christ, or there; believe it not.

For there shall arise false Christs, and false prophets, and shall shew great signs and wonders; insomuch that, if it were possible, they shall deceive the very elect.

According to Jesus, life on planet earth will drastically change at this point in human history. Right in the middle of the Tribulation, Jesus tells us that with this event of the Abomination of Desolation and the rejection of the Antichrist by the Jews, the terror that was simply the Tribulation now becomes the *Great* Tribulation.

Note that Jesus clearly states that this great tribulation will exceed anything that has ever occurred on this planet. It will be so bad, it is difficult for us to imagine. Fortunately, this type of tribulation will never occur again, either.

If we look at the judgments that occurred during the first part of the tribulation, they appear to be horrible enough. Yet what is coming is even worse. This is so because of two reasons:

1. *The Antichrist knows his time is now very short*
2. *He is exceedingly angry over the prospect of the Jews not worshipping him and being able to get away from him*

Since Antichrist is empowered by Satan, his anger is more than simply mortal anger. His anger is fully satanic and the strength that compels him is also satanic.

I can picture a man who sleeps little and eats little, gaining his supernatural power from the enemy of our souls. His one mission is to eradicate *Jews* and all those who oppose him as god. He also knows that Jesus will be returning, and he must do everything he can to stop Him from doing so. If Jesus is able to return, He will be able to claim this earth by reigning from David's throne in Jerusalem. If Jesus does that, the whole thing is over and Antichrist knows it.

So Antichrist begins to craft a plan that will hopefully guarantee his victory over Jesus. He will search the world over and execute all those people who refuse to bow down to him, and he will gather his forces together so that when Jesus makes a move to return to earth, Antichrist with his troops will be ready for Him.

Why does he need to execute as many people as possible who do not worship him? He needs to do this simply because he is angry. More importantly, he believes that if he can eradicate God's people from this planet, there will much less for God to work through on this planet.

Right now, the reason the world is as moral as it is, is due solely to authentic Christians and the fact that the Holy Spirit dwells within them, empowers them, and lives through them. This has a remarkable effect on the citizenry of planet earth.

Why do certain laws in the United States continue to exist in spite of the fact that there are so many liberals who want them overturned? Because of the conservative Christians who believe in a morality that is far higher than anything human beings can manufacture on their own.

As I write this, a recent tragedy in Arizona occurred in which a lunatic gunman attempted to assassinate a member of Congress. He wound up severely wounding her and killing other people standing by listening to her.

Immediately, liberals began pointing fingers at conservatives because of the fact that this lunatic was able to obtain a gun. In fact, many linked him directly with Sarah Palin and the TEA Party because of the metaphors used by them.

What has come out is that this individual had been disturbed for some time even before the TEA Party came to the fore. In fact, he had a problem with this same Congressperson before that fateful day.

What has also come to light is the comments and wishes by many within the liberal arena that many conservatives (specifically named) would die, or be killed. This was not brought to the fore by the liberal media, of course, because they were too busy pointing fingers at conservatives.

The point is that the liberal hates anything that smacks of conservatism. While they are loudly denigrating the 2nd Amendment and all who stand behind it, they are doing the very same thing with the 1st Amendment. They do not want anyone to mess with Roe v. Wade because they say a woman should have the right to do to her body what she wants to do, in spite of that fact that it takes two for a woman to become pregnant. Even with invitro-fertilization, a man's sperm is needed. Woman cannot manufacture it.

I cannot even fathom being a sperm donor, meaning that somewhere I would have a child running around and I would not even know who that child was or in what situation they were living. How absurd is that?

Liberals want conservatives to go away, yet without something to offset liberal demands and desires, this world would go down the tubes far faster than it is doing so now. It is the right that balances out the left and that needs to remain.

Unfortunately, at the midpoint of the Tribulation, when Antichrist desecrates the Temple, liberalism will finally have sway over the entire world, and what they are able to create will literally be hell on earth!

Jesus also talks about the days being "shortened," so we have to wonder what that means. Does it actually mean he is going to make the days shorter, by taking time away? Arnold G. Fruchtenbaum in his book *Footsteps of the Messiah*, as well as other commentators, believe that what this means is that there is a set ending to the Tribulation/Great Tribulation. It will not simply go on without end.

Just as the Tribulation will begin with a specific event (the signing of the covenant) on an exact predetermined day, so will it end in the same manner. Jesus will return to end the whole thing on a day chosen by God alone. In that way, the days will be shortened because that period is not left open-ended. It will come to an end when Jesus ends it.

Notice here that Jesus again refers to false prophets. Here, though, He adds something. He talks about the fact that many people will be taken in by these false prophets because of their ability to perform signs and wonders.

In today's world, an excellent magician captivates a crowd. There are the "ooohs" and "aaaahs." People are astounded and mesmerized, and rightly so, because in most cases we do not know how the magic was actually done. Even though in our minds we understand that it is really done through a combination of sleight of hand and distraction, it is very difficult if not impossible to figure out how if the magician is good enough.

My wife and I were having dinner at a restaurant in Southern California one evening and for entertainment, the restaurant had hired a magician to go from table to table with card tricks and whatnot.

He did his card tricks right there in front of both my wife and I, and as much as I tried watching his hands, I could not figure out how he did what he did! Both my wife and I were absolutely amazed! This is the mark of a good magician.

The false prophets and especially the Antichrist of the Tribulation will be much more than expert magicians. They will have the powers of darkness in their corner and they will be able to perform signs and wonders that will astound the world.

The world will not see a show about how the signs and wonders were performed as we have seen today with the masked magician who stands up and does a very complex trick and then shows how he did it. When the false prophets and the Antichrist work their magic, it will be the dark arts, otherwise known as *magick*. This power will be from hell itself, from the chief of all demons, Satan.

The world will follow. Please note that these false signs and wonders will appear to be so miraculous and authentic that Jesus points out that even the elect would be deceived...*if that were possible*. In other words, that is *not* possible, because God will protect authentic Christians from being taken in by the false signs and wonders. However, this tells us how dramatic these things will be. This is also another point in favor of eternal security because it shows that at all points, God is in charge. He will not allow His children to be bamboozled, just as He will not allow them to walk away from Him...*ever*.

7

INSIDE NORTH KOREA

The National Geographic Documentary, *Inside North Korea* is astounding. In this particular documentary, an eye surgeon from Nepal was given permission to enter North Korea for a humanitarian effort. Because of the way life exists (for many) in North Korea, only the privileged ones get to live in Pyong Yang, and only those individuals have jobs, food, clothing, and homes. These are called the privileged ones, and certainly compared to the rest of North Korea, they are privileged.

Even among the privileged, however, there are poor diets, which can cause cataracts. Cataracts left untreated can and have caused blindness for many there.

It was the doctor's desire to help as many people as he could in the ten days he was given to perform the necessary eye surgeries. It was a relatively simple procedure involving the removal of the clouded cataract and replacing it with a high quality plastic lens.

The doctor wanted to perform 1,000 of these surgeries, which amounted to 100 per day. He was able to reach his goal and 1,000 people regained their sight either in one or both of their eyes thanks to this man.

Unbeknownst to the North Korean government, Lisa Ling and her crew traveled with the doctor under the guise of wanting to film a documentary about this doctor and the people he was able to help.

In spite of this, there were high-ranking people from North Korea who accompanied them everywhere they went. These were referred to as "minders." It was their job to ensure that no rules were broken by the crew.

At one point, one of the crew's photographers took a picture of a very, very tall statue of Kim Il Sung, Kim Il Jong's father. One of the minders chided him because the photographer had to actually lie down on the ground to get a full shot of the statue. He then threatened him with expulsion the next day. That did not occur.

Lisa and her crew were able to go into other places to see what life was like. Of course, there were many places they were not allowed to go or see, so at least some of the footage was used from another documentary. They also used a satellite image of one area of North Korea that housed one of their notorious prison camps. These are simply referred to with a number. This was prison camp number 22 and it held 20,000 people, mostly families.

The way it worked in North Korea was, if you were heard complaining about the monthly rations, or anything that would cause your neighbor or friend to question your loyalty, those neighbors or friends would turn you in to the local authorities. Not only would the local authorities come knocking on your door to haul you off to jail, but your entire family and your extended family was taken as well.

All of you en masse were then taken to one of these camps, where you lived out the rest of your natural life, until you died of old age, disease, or were executed. No one died of old age. The work was grueling, the food was in very short supply, and disease was rampant.

One soldier, who had managed to successfully defect to South Korea and was given asylum, spoke of being a guard in that camp. He said they were trained to not see the people there as human beings. Because of that, the individuals imprisoned in this camp were mistreated horribly, and since they were no longer considered to be "people," abuse and execution were the normal conditions that existed in the camp.

He related one incidence in which several children found a kernel of corn in a pile of cow dung. Because they were so hungry, they fought over it, and one eventually washed it and ate it.

All throughout the documentary, the dictator of North Korea was praised. He could do no wrong, and to the North Korean people, he was/is a god. Anything good that came into their lives was due solely to Kim Il Jong and his father before him. Anything bad that came their way was because they needed to try harder.

In every home (that Lisa was allowed to enter) there were no pictures or photos on the wall, except for Kim Il Sung and Kim Il Jong. Each member of the family would bow and praise their leaders (past and present) on a daily basis and often throughout the day.

Of course, it goes without saying that the children were taught from a very young age that Kim Il Jong is god and Americans (and other outsiders) are evil. The unity in North Korea exists because both Kims brought the people together as a united front against all outsiders, who were and are considered to be enemies of North Korea.

At the end of all of the doctor's surgeries, he went through to each patient as they waited and removed their bandages. One by one, they volunteered that they could now see. Many of them had no sight for many years. Interestingly enough, the first thing every patient did was not thank the doctor who physically gave them their sight, but instead went and bowed before the portraits of both Kims.

Each patient lifted hands high in boisterous praise to their "dear leader" who had cared about them to give them back their eyesight. Many were overcome with emotion as they considered how kind and thoughtful their dear leader was to even be aware of their existence.

As I pondered this documentary, I could not help but make a comparison between North Korea's godless dictator and the final world dictator who will demand worship and will call himself God, just as Paul says he will do in 2 Thessalonians 2. This coming world dictator will consider no one but himself. The lives of others will mean nothing to him. They are a means to the end and the end is the eradication of all who oppose his alleged deity, as well as to stop Jesus Christ before He returns to earth.

The day is coming when the Tribulation (the first 3.5 years) and the Great Tribulation (the second 3.5 years) will wreak havoc on an unsuspecting world, just like the flood of Noah's day did and the fire and brimstone of Lot's day did. Out of the mire and mess, one man will stand up above the crowd and will make promises he does not keep. His mouth will be filled with his own praise and the populace will believe him.

The entire world will follow after this coming man of sin. They will become enraptured with this man, sold out to him either out of love and loyalty or abject fear.

> *"And the ten horns out of this kingdom are ten kings that shall arise: and another shall rise after them; and he shall be diverse from the first, and he shall subdue three kings.*
>
> *"And he shall speak great words against the most High, and shall wear out the saints of the most High, and think to change times and laws: and they shall be given into his hand until a time and times and the dividing of time."*
> Daniel 7:24-25

In the above two verses we read about a time when the world will have collapsed into a one-world government. From that point, I'm assuming to make it easier to rule over people, this one-world will be divided up into ten realms, each with one person in charge of that section.

By the way, if you believe this to be far-fetched, I'd recommend doing a search on the *Club of Rome*. A number of years ago, this group of the world's elite did much the same thing, dividing the world up (on paper) into ten manageable sections. I'm not saying that the Club of Rome's plan is the one that will go into effect. I'm simply saying that it's already be bandied about by the world's elite.

Notice though that after the world is divided up into ten sections, "*another shall rise after them.*" This "another" is none other than the Antichrist himself. It is interesting, is it not, that the Antichrist waits until the world has had some sort of collapse or some other cataclysmic event that causes it to become one?

Even at that, the Antichrist bides his time. He makes no move yet. It is only when the world is divided up into ten parts that he makes his move to the top. Why? I believe it's because when the world is divided up into ten parcels, with an individual over each, it becomes far easier for the Antichrist to put his plan of world domination in motion.

Can you see it? Here the world goes along and the elitists finally get what they want; absolute control over the world and its citizenry. Are they happy campers or what? They are now in a position to do anything they want to do. The problem is, of course, that they had not counted on the fact that someone else will rise up from among their ranks and usurp their power.

This is exactly what he does. Notice the text also states that this "another" comes to the fore after the first ten kings, and that he is different from those ten kings. He also subdues three of the ten. I imagine at this point he kills three kings in order to take over those three areas.

This does a couple of things. It shows everyone that though they *thought* they had finally arrived with no one to answer to, they were wrong. It also shows them that this Antichrist is not above killing to get his way. His coup pays off because it is obvious that the remaining seven kings put up no struggle at all. In fact, for the time being, they are allowed to continue their hold over their own 1/10th of the world...with Antichrist's permission. This means that these elitists, who looked forward to the day when they would have enough power to no longer worry about the average citizen and who firmly believed that when that day came they would answer to no one except themselves, were wrong.

They now find themselves in the very awkward position of being an elitist who must answer to someone else, and the guy they have to answer to has no qualms about killing any or all of them in his effort to grab power. The remaining seven opt to play along since they really do not want to die at this point.

The next paragraph of Daniel that I quoted above highlights something that is abysmally interesting because of its blasphemous nature. Notice that the Antichrist's rise to power includes killing three leaders. Once he arrived at a spot in which he felt secure in his own position, he really began to let his hair down.

The world begins to see the inner psychoses of this person as he uses his bully pulpit to brag about himself for all he's worth. Like Satan of old, the Antichrist takes every opportunity to puff himself up before the entire world, making himself more important and more powerful than God Himself!

The phrase "a time and times and the dividing of time," or another way you may have heard it is "a time, times, and half a time," literally means 42 months, or 3.5 years. Because of this, many believe that the Tribulation will only last for 3.5 years then, not the seven that we've heard so much about.

This is not what the text is saying. If we consider the Bible as a whole, allowing Scripture to interpret Scripture, the entire Tribulation period lasts for a full seven years. We know this from Daniel 9:24-27. Verse 27 specifically states that he will enter into a covenant with the many for one week. We know that the term "week" or "weeks" in this entire chapter's context is ultimately referencing years. Context is important.

If that is true then why is it that Daniel 7 and parts of Revelation refer merely to a 3.5 year period? They do and they don't. Please note that in Revelation 6, the very first seal to open is the one which sends the rider on the horse across the landscape. While some believe this white rider is Jesus (heaven forbid!), it can't be since Jesus does not return until the end of the Tribulation. This particular white rider is not wearing a kingly crown either. He is simply wearing a *stephanos* or victory crown. Jesus wears a diadem crown. Big difference.

So in essence, Antichrist is "let out" the very first part of the Tribulation. That makes sense since Daniel 9:27 speaks of the fact that the final week begins when the "he" in that verse signs a covenant with "the many" for one week. People often get confused about this verse and the numerous uses of "he" in Daniel 9:24-27. It's not confusing at all if we keep in mind the law of antecedents. The "he" in verse 27 has to be referring back to the very last use of "he," and that "he" is not talking about Jesus. It is talking not about "the" Prince, but "a" prince who is of the people who destroyed the Temple and Jerusalem (the prince of the people who is to come).

So if the Antichrist kicks off the Tribulation with the event of signing the covenant with Israel for the last week, this has to be a period of seven years. The entire week is seven years and this covenant starts the tribulation. It starts getting really bad when the Antichrist goes into the rebuilt Temple and desecrates it. That begins the "great tribulation" that Jesus speaks of in Matthew 24:21. It is because of the desolation created by the Antichrist that the Jews are forced to flee to the hills.

Because the Jews flee, the Antichrist becomes extremely angry! In fact, he is so angry that he cannot get at these Jews, he goes after Christians instead! The Antichrist's rise to power happens before the beginning of the Tribulation period and the reason why is obvious. He apparently has the authority to act on behalf of the world in creating and offering a covenant with Israel that will guarantee them "peace and safety" so that they can begin building their Temple and reestablish their sacrificial system. They would not need to rebuild much of it before they could begin the sacrificial system, either.

So prior to the beginning of the Tribulation, the following things mush occur:

1. the world becomes a united one-world government
2. the world is then divided into ten regions

3. one leader is placed over each region
4. the Antichrist, who is not one of those original ten leaders, subdues three
5. the Antichrist takes power from the other seven remaining leaders, allowing them to retain their positions in exchange for their loyalty

This must be in place prior to the beginning of the Tribulation in order for the Antichrist to be positioned to act on behalf of the world to broker peace in the Middle East. Once the Tribulation begins, it certainly seems as though the Antichrist is quiet, relatively speaking. We do not hear from him until the middle part of the Tribulation when he desecrates the Temple. Outsmarted, he goes on a rampage against any and all who refuse to worship him.

So is the Antichrist remaining silent during the first part of the Tribulation? I cannot imagine it. I see him as putting all the pieces of the puzzle together as he climbs to the top.

It is impossible for us know what goes on inside the dictatorship of Kim Il Jong, yet it is clear that he is in charge of that country and rules it with an iron fist. The decisions he makes behind closed doors are not available for the world to see until after his decisions are carried out.

Let's not forget that the entire Tribulation is God's wrath being poured out on the world. Because of that, the focus is not the Antichrist. It is God and the judgments He uses to bring humanity to its knees. Just because we do not read about the Antichrist during the first 3.5 years does not mean that he is not there, or that he is not doing anything.

I believe that he will be spending the first 3.5 years getting all his ducks in a row so that when the time comes the world will see him as he wants to be seen; as savior, god, and lord. The world will at this time be encouraged to give their respect, loyalty, and even their worship to the Antichrist. Those that do will be rewarded, just as those in North Korea are rewarded for their loyalty to Kim Il Jong.

However, at the midpoint, when the Antichrist unveils himself to the Jews, what was previously recommended will then become mandatory on pain of death.

Life in North Korea is cheap; very cheap. It takes only one small mistake to be tossed into a prison camp. For those who are "privileged," it takes only one small mistake to be executed. North Korea is a small-scale picture of what life will be like on a worldwide scale during the Tribulation.

There will be no second chances for people during that time. You will either bow to the Antichrist or lose your life. Only authentic Christians would willingly give up their lives instead of bowing to Satan. Many others will lose their lives for political reasons.

The most tragic thing I noted while watching the documentary was how willingly everyone bowed to and praised Kim Il Jong. Certainly, many did it out of fear - but maybe not. The entire country had been brainwashed for so many generations that they knew nothing else. Cell phones are not allowed. The news is carefully selected and broadcast only with the permission of Kim Il Jong. In essence, the people of North Korea lived in what Lisa Ling rightly terms the hermit world. They know nothing of anything outside the borders of North Korea. They have no clue. To them, countries and people outside North Korea are enemies and they should not only be repudiated, but if given the opportunity, killed as enemies.

During the time of the Tribulation, I cannot imagine how bad it will be. Watching *Inside North Korea* provides a glimpse of a godless dictator who has accepted the title of god. The "dear leader" of North Korea is loved by young and old in that country. They really have no choice in the matter. To react in any other way toward Jong means certain death. Such is the way of dictators, and if we can imagine that 100 or 1,000 times worse, that is what we will have with the Antichrist.

Folks, people need the Lord. They need to be introduced to Him long before the Tribulation begins. We have a job and we must take it seriously. Every area of our lives should mirror Christ. Every area.

I recently opted to place bumper stickers that have a Christian message on my car. It is too easy for me to give into frustration while driving. People cut you off, do not use blinkers, will not let you in their lane and many other things besides. With bumper stickers I am forced to consider my Christianity. I am forced to remember that God is in charge of my life. I am forced to give myself to Him during those frustrating times when someone does something selfish or stupid behind the wheel that causes a problem for me.

We have an obligation to tell the world about salvation in Jesus. With that comes the requirement that our life equals our talk. We need to pray for one another that we can be the people God wants us to be, in a world that is increasingly walking away from Him.

Just as the doctor in the documentary went on a mission to give people their sight back, we need to be on a mission to introduce people to the Light of this world (cf. John 9). Once they see this Light, they will never be in darkness again. Physical sight is certainly good. I'm glad I have it and I'll bet you are glad you have it too. However, spiritual sight is infinitely better.

HELL BREAKS LOOSE

Following verse 25, the Lord begins to wrap things up, yet there is still a major roller coaster ride (and not a good one) for the people of earth. If we remember that Antichrist's main goal is to *be* God on earth, we then understand why he needs to keep Jesus from returning.

This next part of the period known as the Tribulation is actually referred to as the Great Tribulation by our Lord. He refers to it as such simply because of how bad things are going to become. If we compare the Olivet Discourse with parts of Revelation, it is quickly clear that this is no picnic. In fact, though life was worth pretty much nothing to the Antichrist *before* he defiled the Temple, it is worth less than nothing now. His goal is to muster all his supernatural energy and his earthly troops and prepare for the battle ahead: Armageddon. This is when the Lord will physically return to set up His Kingdom on the earth. There is a legal reason why He must do this, aside from the fact that He has promised He will and many prophecies have been made about this event and following.

Matthew 24:26-28
Wherefore if they shall say unto you, Behold, he is in the desert; go not forth: behold, he is in the secret chambers; believe it not.

For as the lightning cometh out of the east, and shineth even unto the west; so shall also the coming of the Son of man be.

For wheresoever the carcase is, there will the eagles be gathered together.

The above verses are interesting because Jesus again takes the time to point out the fact that false prophets will be prevalent and they should be avoided at all costs. Not only this, but obviously there will be false rumors about Jesus returning. We have those same false rumors today, with Harold Camping and others who believe that in spite of the fact that Jesus said no one would know the day or hour of His return, that is not what He really meant.

So we can see that there will be this sense during this point in the Tribulation when people will be desperate for the Lord to return. However, Jesus is making it clear that His second return will *not* be secret like His first advent when He clothed Himself with humanity.

This second coming of Jesus will be seen by every eye. When lightning shines in the night sky, it literally lights up the entire sky and is seen by everyone in that vicinity. I recall my days as a youth living in Hobart, NY, a town of less than 1,000 people. It was quaint, although small towns have their problems. As a kid, I enjoyed it because there was so much to occupy me, whether it was riding my bike, hiking, or just fishing in the Delaware River, which I did much of the time. It was kind of like a Mark Twain-type of village which he describes in Huckleberry Finn or Tom Sawyer.

At any rate, in preparing for fishing, I would often go out at night just after it rained and get the many nightwalkers that came to the surface of the ground. It was during one of these times that the rain had not completely stopped, but I thought it was good to go out and start collecting worms for fishing. While bent over, looking at the ground for any worms that had popped up to the surface, a huge sound of thunder clapped across the sky. Shortly after that came the lightning, and that lightning literally caused the entire sky to turn to daylight for a brief second or two.

This is the way it will be when Jesus returns. His return will break out onto the sky even if it is the middle of the day, just as the light of Jesus' presence on the road to Damascus was far brighter than the sun (cf. Acts 9) when Saul was converted to Christianity and became the apostle Paul. "Every eye will see Him" could happen literally by the brightness of His presence alone, which would reverberate around the entire globe; or with the technology in place today, every eye will see Him instantly from wherever they happen to be located.

In essence, the world will see the *return* of the rightful Owner of this planet, and the results of that will not be pretty for some. In the meantime, Antichrist needs to hustle to put his plans into action so that he is prepared for one of the major events since Creation.

It is interesting that Jesus follows up the statement about His visible return with a reference to a carcass and carrion birds. When understood within this context, it is not at all strange, though.

When Jesus returns, He will set everything right. In order to do that, He will judge the people of the nations. This is essentially what is occurring within the context of the Sheep and the Goats parable (cf. Matthew 25:31-46).

In the Sheep and the Goats parable, the sheep represent the righteous and the goats the unrighteous. That is clear from the context. Notice that both groups are judged on the basis of what they did. This is a bit deceiving at first glance because it tends to make people think of the fact that it is *works* that grants us eternal life. When compared to the rest of Scripture, we know this cannot be true because there are too many places where the Bible teaches that salvation is by grace *only* and there is nothing we can do to earn it.

If that is the case, then why the emphasis on various works here? We have mentioned this before, but it is good to repeat important facts. Please note that the righteous did all kinds of things in their lives (especially during the tribulation period) of which they were not even aware they had done. This is evidenced by their questions "When did we do that, or this, Lord?"

What the righteous did, they did *naturally* because they were authentic Christians. Authentic Christians do things from the heart. They do not do these things to be noticed by people, and because it is a natural outflow of their inner Christianity, it is not something that they notice themselves doing.

The unsaved do not live like this. They do things for *show*, and because they are done for show, they are very well aware of the fact that they are doing them. Beyond this, they will not do things that are not noticed by others. Visiting prisoners, feeding the sick and clothing the needy are things that generally do not receive a good deal of fanfare. Because of that, people who want and need attention for their works will not choose those things that are out of the limelight.

In this particular case, there is another important point to consider here. Note that Jesus is the Judge, and He specifically notes that these things were either done or not done to *Him*. Why? It is because if they were done to the least of His brothers (Jews), they were done to Him.

In essence, it appears that this judgment by Christ is predicated upon how people looked out for and cared for Jews during the Tribulation. This is specifically noteworthy considering the fact that during the Second World War virtually no one helped Jews who were daily being slaughtered by Nazi Germany. There were certainly a few who helped by hiding Jews in their attics or behind false walls, but by and large, almost no one paid any attention to these individuals who were killed by the thousands daily.

During the Tribulation, the Antichrist will lead another extermination attempt, and because of this Jesus will judge people based on how they treated His brothers, the Jews. Again, only those authentic Christians during this time will have the fortitude, the wherewithal and the desire to help Jews who are being hounded by the Antichrist. This will take tremendous courage on the part of the Christians because it will mean that they will possibly come under fire themselves.

People who are not Christians will not bother, and it is clear from this parable that this is the case. This is a fact of life. It is difficult enough for Christians to do what is right all the time. During persecution – and the Tribulation will have plenty of persecution to go around – the sheep will literally be separated from the goats not only *after* the Tribulation, but during it. Selfish people normally do things that benefit *self*. This is true now and will be even truer during this coming horrific period of time.

The situation resulting from judgment will bring about tremendous death to multitudes of people. As they are judged by Christ, they will die and their souls will leave their physical bodies in death. The pile of dead will build up and provide food for carrion for months.

It is a well known fact that during each year, millions of carrion fly through and stop at Israel. As far back as 2004, there was an increase in and affection for carrion birds that seemed to thrive in Israel. Carrion serves a purpose; a necessary purpose. It is also interesting to note that carrion – birds of prey – are not kosher, but all other birds that do not fall into the category of carrion *are* kosher. The carrion that will exist during the time of the sheep and the goats judgment will be perfectly suited to feed on the carcasses of the dead.

Matthew 24:29-31
Immediately after the tribulation of those days shall the sun be darkened, and the moon shall not give her light, and the stars shall fall from heaven, and the powers of the heavens shall be shaken:

And then shall appear the sign of the Son of man in heaven: and then shall all the tribes of the earth mourn, and they shall see the Son of man coming in the clouds of heaven with power and great glory.

And he shall send his angels with a great sound of a trumpet, and they shall gather together his elect from the four winds, from one end of heaven to the other.

In the above verses, Jesus points out that when the seven-year Tribulation has ended, there will be a few signs in the sky. These signs act as the house lights going off just prior to the curtain going up. Notice that the sun will be darkened and the moon will not be visible. This makes sense, of course, because the moon's light is merely light reflected from the sun.

In addition to these dramatic signs, the stars will fall from the sky and the powers of the heavens will literally shake. I can imagine a huge ominous thunder clap or two (or three) as the earth prepares to receive the rightful Owner of this planet, Jesus Himself.

Once these signs in the heavens have gotten everyone's attention, the sign of the Son of Man will appear. That sign is none other than the appearance of Jesus Himself. The text tells us that all the tribes of the earth will mourn, and rightly so. More than one commentator has pointed out that the use of the word "tribes" here cannot simply mean those national tribes of Israel. The picture we are getting here is that the entire world will witness this spectacle, both the signs preceding Jesus' appearance, and His appearance itself.

Try to imagine a world that is on the verge of destroying itself. People and nations are preoccupied with their own self-created problems. They are essentially godless and evil and have no time for God. In fact, by this point in the Tribulation, the only god most will worship is the Antichrist.

When Jesus – the *only* real God – breaks through the skies and into the earthly realm, though much of the world will be quite surprised by His presence (since they did not believe He existed), the Antichrist knew that Jesus would one day return. This is exactly why the Antichrist spent so much time clawing his way to the top, and once there, gathering his earthly troops together. He plans on stopping Jesus before He touches down on the Mount of Olives. This is the final battle, the battle known as Armageddon, because it occurs on the Plain of Megiddo in Israel.

As it turns out, it is not much of a battle at all, because Scripture tells us that Jesus will destroy the Antichrist with the breath of His mouth. In other words, Jesus will destroy the Antichrist with a word. Paul tells us, *"And then shall that Wicked be revealed, whom the Lord shall consume with the spirit of his mouth, and shall destroy with the brightness of his coming"* (2 Thessalonians 2:8). For Antichrist, the battle is over before it starts.

Notice at this point, upon Jesus' return, the Lord's angels will gather the elect from all parts of the earth. Not only does judgment occur with terrible results for the wicked, but the righteous living on the earth will be rewarded at this point as well.

Once the Antichrist defiles the rebuilt Jewish Temple, what follows is three and a half years of literal hell on earth. (For more on this, it is suggested that the reader pick up a copy of *The End of the Ages*, a commentary for the layperson also by the author of this book.) The Tribulation comes to its pre-ordained end when Jesus literally parts the skies and touches down on planet earth. It is at that point that the righteousness of Christ will affect the entire earth and those who reside here. Is this all some fairy tale or pie in the sky dream? Not if the Bible has any merit at all. There is good reason to believe that the Bible has tremendous veracity simply because of all the prophecies that have taken place years after they were first uttered.

Each person is responsible for their own particular view or understanding of Jesus and the Bible. It is not something that anyone should take lightly, yet unfortunately, all too many people put off coming to any real decision. The truth of the matter is that this in itself is a decision. Ignorance is no excuse, and God will hold each of us responsible for the decisions we make in this life. The truth of the matter is that there is no more important decision a person can make than that revolving around the true identity of Jesus and the Bible that He is said to have written.

9

A BREAK IN THE ACTION

At this point in the narrative, there is a bit of a parenthesis as Jesus provides a simple illustration to His disciples. The point of the illustration is for the disciples to recognize that it will be easy to discern when these things will occur if they simply pay attention. Just as they are able to understand the changing of the seasons because of the way the trees change, so will they be able to discern the times of the age...if they are paying attention.

Matthew 24:32-33
Now learn a parable of the fig tree; When his branch is yet tender, and putteth forth leaves, ye know that summer is nigh:

So likewise ye, when ye shall see all these things, know that it is near, even at the doors."

Jesus points out that when His disciples begin to see the things occur that He has described, it can be taken as a strong indication that things are drawing to a close.

Matthew 24:34-35
Verily I say unto you, This generation shall not pass, till all these things be fulfilled.

Heaven and earth shall pass away, but my words shall not pass away.

The above verse contains one of the most controversial and most often argued about phrases in all of the study of Eschatology. Jesus says *"this generation shall not pass."* There has been plenty of discussion regarding what that means. Some take it to mean the generation that Jesus lived in, so in that case, He would have meant that everything He had just discussed would come true in that generation.

Others take it to mean the generation that is living when all the things that Jesus discusses comes to pass. In that case, He would of necessity be referring to the very last generation before He physically returns to the earth to set up His Messianic Kingdom.

Can we know for sure? I believe we can. We should always approach God's Word through prayer. The trouble is that after people arrive at a decision, they then often begin to see those who have arrived at a varying opinion as "false teachers."

People who believe one thing while strongly feeling that other people who believe something else entirely are wrong often go to the extreme of labeling those with whom they disagree as false teachers, or false prophets. The implication then is that the person teaching the falsehood is not even *saved*.

This is ludicrous. There is *nothing* in Scripture that implies or teaches that a person's salvation hinges on their viewpoint about Eschatology (and remember, Eschatology is the study of the end times). The most we can say is that those who do not believe in the physical Second Coming of Jesus to this earth have questionable beliefs.

It is not up to us to decide who is and who is not saved because of their view of Eschatology. It is not even up to us to determine who is and who is not saved because we may *think* that they are not saved. That is God's department. While we can certainly see things in brothers and sisters that are not right, we need to be careful about labeling people unsaved. This does not mean we turn a blind eye to egregious situations in another person's life. It simply means that we do not judge that person because of those situations.

There is one big exception here, though. When dealing with people who actually do teach and believe a false salvation message, it is incumbent upon us to instruct them. For instance, if someone teaches that salvation is by grace *plus works*, as a number of groups do (Jehovah's Witnesses, Mormons, Seventh-day Adventists, etc.), we would be remiss if we do not seek to gently correct them.

To show that they are incorrect, we might turn to the pages of Ephesians 2, which tells us that salvation is by grace alone, not of works, in order to keep us from boasting (cf. Ephesians 2:8-10). There are other places we can take them in Scripture as well, such as Romans chapters eight, nine, and ten. These texts clearly point out that salvation is not based on anything we do. It is all God's work.

In other words, unlike Eschatology, salvation is the most important message we can share with others. A right or wrong view of Eschatology does not save a person. Salvation is the only thing that saves a person, and while it might be interesting or even entertaining to discuss aspects of Eschatology, too often it breaks down into quarrels that have absolutely no benefit at all.

Getting back to the *"this generation shall not pass,"* we must ask ourselves what Jesus meant by that statement. The main reasons I take that statement to refer to the very last generation prior to the Lord's physical return are the following:

1. *Jesus has essentially just finished explaining the entire timeline leading <u>up to and including the end of the age</u>.*
2. *Jesus is now wrapping things up and tying everything together for His listeners.*
3. *Jesus has already discussed the fact that He has already returned and the elect throughout the world will be gathered (cf. vv. 30-31).*
4. *He has spoken of His physical return to this earth, not a sort of spiritual return as some believe occurred in A.D. 70.*

It is difficult for me to take His statement – *this generation shall not pass* – any other way except to mean the very last generation living just before He returns. I realize, of course, that there are numerous opinions about this passage. Some take it to mean that all the things Jesus spoke of would occur during that generation alive at the time He provided this information.

The difficulty, though, is that in order for that to be true, the text of Scripture needs to be allegorized and logic needs to be tossed out. In other words, what does it mean when He speaks of His personal, physical return to the earth? Matthew 24:30 states very clearly the following: *"And then shall appear the sign of the Son of man in heaven: and then shall all the tribes of the earth mourn, and they shall see the Son of man coming in the clouds of heaven with power and great glory."* We can take this statement one of two ways. We can take it literally or figuratively (allegorically).

If we take Jesus' words figuratively, then we are free to apply a spiritual meaning to the text. We can then say, for instance, as some do, that Jesus returned *spiritually* in A.D. 70 when God judged Israel by using the Romans to destroy Jerusalem and the Temple, just as Jesus said would occur (cf. Matthew 24:2). In that verse of Matthew, Jesus alludes to the time in the future when no stone would stand upon another. In other words, the entire Temple edifice would be destroyed. God *did* this as judgment on the entire nation of Israel. This in fact occurred in A.D. 70.

But can we also accurately state that this is when Jesus "returned" to the earth at the end of the age? We can only say that if we understand Scripture in *figurative* terms. How do we know that when Jesus referred to His own return to earth that He was *not* speaking figuratively, but was in fact speaking in literal terms?

If we go to the first chapter of Acts, we read the words, *"why stand ye gazing up into heaven? this same Jesus, which is taken up from you into heaven, shall so come in like manner as ye have seen him go into heaven"* (Acts 1:11). In this particular situation, Jesus had just ascended to heaven after spending forty days with His disciples *after* He had been resurrected.

As He is taken up to heaven, the disciples standing there who witnessed the event were obviously and understandably confused and excited. Had they really seen their Master ascend into heaven? Had Jesus been caught up to the clouds and taken out of their sight?

As they stood there, staring up into the sky, just as we would have done, two angels appeared and essentially brought the men back to earth by asking them a question and making a statement. The question was: *why are you staring up into the sky?* The statement was: *Jesus will return this very same way you saw Him leave.* How can there be another meaning to that statement, as some suggest?

Here then we see that the two angels are telling the disciples that Jesus will physically return to the earth one day. There is really no other way to understand that text without taking it figuratively.

However, taking the Scriptures figuratively when there is no reason to do so is dangerous, simply because it allows us then to take the meaning of Scripture any way we want to take it.

God wrote the Bible and He used over forty human authors to do it, in the space of roughly 1,600 years. He did this mainly to authenticate His message. The consistency in the Bible is uncanny, and the fact that it was written by that many human beings over the course of sixteen centuries proves the veracity of the Bible.

The main thing we need to keep in mind as we approach Scripture is that it is God's Word to humanity. Because it is His Word to us, then we need to do everything possible to gain *His* meaning from His Word. We cannot approach His Word deciding that we will take this figuratively and that literally at whim.

We are dealing with God's Word. As such, we need to be concerned that we are not doing damage to the Scriptures by reading into it because of some faulty method of interpretation we have chosen to use. We are responsible for the way we understand the Bible.

If I wrote you a letter, you would be required to understand what I meant when I wrote it. You are not free to indiscriminately place your meaning over my words. You are obligated to discern my meaning so that you will understand what I have said to you. Applying figurative meaning to parts of my letter when there is no reason to do so is wrong because you will undoubtedly come away with a meaning that I did not intend for you to gain. How much more should we respect God's Word, approaching it with humility and caution lest we apply a wrong meaning to His Word through faulty interpretive methods?

So what do we have? We have the testimony of two angels in Acts 1 telling us that Jesus would return the exact same way the disciples saw Him go. The simple question then is: *has that taken place yet?*

Well, if Jesus has returned, I missed it and so did you. In fact, if He did return, we know that what Jesus said did not come true. He said it would occur at the end of the age. Has that end come and gone? Has it?

You will recall that Jesus said these words about His own future return to earth:

"For as the lightning cometh out of the east, and shineth even unto the west; so shall also the coming of the Son of man be" (Matthew 24:27).

"Immediately after the tribulation of those days shall the sun be darkened, and the moon shall not give her light, and the stars shall fall from heaven, and the powers of the heavens shall be shaken:

"And then shall appear the sign of the Son of man in heaven: and then shall all the tribes of the earth mourn, and they shall see the Son of man coming in the clouds of heaven with power and great glory" (Matthew 24:29-30).

Again, if we consider Jesus' words in light of the pronouncement of the angels in Acts 1, what is being described is the *physical, bodily, visual* return of Jesus to this earth. It can be nothing else. If this is the case, then of necessity, when Jesus said *this generation shall not pass*, He had to be referring to the generation alive just before He physically returns. How can it be anything else? Jesus not only spoke about "this generation," but He also spoke of the "end of the age." These two go hand in hand. Jesus will return at the end of the age and the generation living then will experience all of it.

There are people today who allegorize the Bible so much with respect to prophecy that they have come to believe that Jesus will not physically return to the earth. These people are in the category of being *Amillennialists* because they do not believe in the physical, one-thousand-year reign of Jesus on this earth at some point in the future. In my opinion, their viewpoint or interpretation does a great deal of damage to the text of Scripture. It takes what appears to be obvious and turns it into something that has an opposite meaning.

After stating *this generation shall not pass away*, He goes one step further and vouchsafes His own pronouncement by stating without equivocation, "*heaven and earth shall pass away, but my words shall not pass away*" (Matthew 24:35).

Because Jesus says that, it is even more important for us to rightly understand what He is saying. If Scripture that we have quoted means anything, we know that He will physically return one day to rule for one-thousand years. If He is going to actually and physically return, then the reference to "this generation" of necessity must refer to the generation living just prior to His physical return. It does not make sense any other way.

To wrap this up, please note again the verse in Matthew 24 that states, "*Verily I say unto you, This generation shall not pass, **till all these things be fulfilled***" (Matthew 24:34; emphasis mine). It is not merely that Jesus says "this generation shall not pass," but the fact that He *adds to it* the words "till all these things be fulfilled." The plain meaning of that is that everything He has just stated will be fulfilled with "this generation," the generation He referred to that will be alive *at the end of the age just prior to His physical return.*

Has everything been fulfilled yet? No, because the biggest event in that entire litany of events of Matthew 24 is the physical return of Jesus. Since that event has not occurred, then we can clearly discern that He could *not* have been referring to the generation alive when He was alive just prior to His death, resurrection, and ascension. In short, Jesus had to have been referring to the generation that was alive just before He physically returns to this earth.

10

NO GUESSING PLEASE

While it is clear that not all things have been fulfilled yet, it is equally clear that no one will know when Jesus will return. This has not stopped some from making their best guess.

Matthew 24:36-37
But of that day and hour knoweth no man, no, not the angels of heaven, but my Father only. But as the days of Noah were, so shall also the coming of the Son of man be.

Jesus is still discussing His physical return and now He qualifies it by stating that no one will know the day or hour. Why did He say this?

I'm sure He said it because He knew that people would try to be making guesses about His return.

The guessing game of when Jesus will return has been played throughout history and it is still being played. Most recently, a man named Harold Camping of Family Radio has decided that Jesus will be returning on May 21, 2011. Harold Camping has previously named a date in 1994 and was shocked to discover that he was wrong. He now states that he got the math wrong, which brought him to this latest guess of May 21, 2011. Will he be correct this time? The short answer to that is *no*. If Camping is by some freak chance correct, it will be pure *luck*.

Jesus said that no one would know the day or hour. Camping says that the day is going to be May 21, 2011. Who is correct? Obviously, Jesus is correct since He is God and God cannot lie (Titus 1:2; Hebrews 6:18). Besides, we already know that Camping was in error

when he made his first guess in the 90s. His track record is not good, so there is no reason to think that he is correct this time.

Unfortunately, people *do* believe Harold Camping. This is all too clear, and that tells me something. It tells me that people do not read the Bible for themselves. They take what someone like Harold Camping says and simply go with it, without doing the research on it. If they took the time to research it, they would conclude that unless Jesus is lying, no one will know the day or hour.

After stating that no one will know the day or hour (except Harold Camping apparently), Jesus then compares the day of His return with the days of Noah. It is important then to understand what was going on during Noah's day so that we can understand what things will be like during the time just before Jesus' return.

Matthew 24:38-39
For as in the days that were before the flood they were eating and drinking, marrying and giving in marriage, until the day that Noe entered into the ark,

And knew not until the flood came, and took them all away; so shall also the coming of the Son of man be.

We see we do not have to guess about Jesus' meaning. He references Noah's day and then explains what He means. He says that during the time of Noah, people ate, drank, married, gave their daughters in marriage and essentially did the things that happen in everyday life. In other words, things seemed pretty normal in Noah's day, with people doing very normal things. Of course, we then need to remind ourselves why God chose to destroy the world with a flood, and the answer for us is in Genesis 6:11-13. Here we read that everything about the world had been corrupted, and the only thing humanity thought about was evil. People during Noah's time only wanted to do evil things, yet they also did very normal things.

Jesus is saying that the people of Noah's time lived their lives as if God did not exist. They chose to ignore Him and they did whatever seemed good to them, in spite of the fact that everything they did was completely evil.

Because people had chosen to ignore God, they were not at all ready when God told Noah and his family to enter the Ark. After they entered the Ark, God shut the door and sealed it from the outside (cf. Genesis 7:16). The people outside the Ark perished. They chose to live lives that ignored God and they opted to disbelieve God even though they could see the Ark that Noah was building.

The people of Noah's day saw the sign of the end of the earth, which was the Ark. They saw it being built over a period of 120 years and in spite of that sign, they chose to ignore it. Because they ignored it, they died when the flood waters came.

Jesus is saying that it will be the same just prior to His return. There will be signs, but most people will ignore them. They will simply decide that all the signs are simply coincidental, nothing more than the cycles of life.

We have talked about nine birth pangs that Jesus said would occur before He returned. It is this author's belief that only three of them have occurred up to this point. What are you going to do with those three birth pangs, or signs? Are you going to ignore them, believing that they are simply coincidence, or are you going to consider the fact that God has sent you warnings about what is coming?

The people of Noah's day had no excuse because they saw the Ark being built. They probably had opportunity to talk with Noah, and he would have told them why he was building the Ark. They chose to laugh and not believe. The result of that was death.

In Luke 17, Jesus speaks about much the same thing, but includes the days of Lot as well. You may recall that Lot lived in Sodom, and together with Gomorrah, these twin cities were destroyed by God with fire and brimstone.

The same situation existed in these two cities that existed in Noah's day. People ate, drank, partied, were married, gave daughters away in marriage, and essentially did what we do. There was also a great deal of evil that existed right alongside the normalcy of life. So it is today as well.

We have seen a tremendous increase in terrorism and crime in general. We will never forget 9/11 and the deaths that occurred through the events that took place on that day. Yet we continue with life, eating, drinking, marrying, working, and the rest. Do we stop to consider that the world is not becoming a better place in which to live, but it is becoming far worse?

Today, God has given us signs. He would like very much for us to believe Him since He cannot lie and has never lied. What will you do with those birth pang signs? Just as destruction came upon those who chose not to believe Noah and those who chose not to believe Lot, the Lord's physical return will take the world largely unaware. People will simply not be ready for that event, in spite of the signs He has provided for us.

Why does He provide the signs at all? Why not just take us by surprise and be done with it? It is simply because God loves us and does not want anyone to die without first being in relationship with Him. This is the most important decision any person living on this planet can make before they die. Jesus explained this carefully to a Pharisee named Nicodemus in John 3. He told Nicodemus that unless a person becomes born again, or born from above, they will not see the Kingdom of God (experience eternal life). Being born again is a spiritual transaction that occurs when a person trusts in Jesus and the work He did on our behalf.

What did Jesus do? He lived a sinless life, and at the end of His life, though He was betrayed by people He knew, He willingly gave His life up, dying a most brutal death in order that our sins – yours and mine – would be fully paid for by the action of His death.

After His death, He rose from the grave because the grave could not hold Him. His perfection was something that would not – could not – decay, and death had no hold over Him. His resurrection sealed the deal and defeated Satan.

Satan wants nothing more than for you to choose to disbelieve God. Satan knows that if you die without ever having believed in who Jesus is and what He accomplished for you, you will not spend eternity with God, but you will spend eternity separated from God. That is not a wonderful prospect.

You must understand and believe the truth. The truth will literally set you free from death and hell (cf. John 8:32). You have the obligation to make a decision about Jesus and His life, death, and resurrection. You cannot simply put it off because by doing that, you have made a decision that you will not accept the truth about Jesus.

God has graciously given us signs, just as He gave signs to the people in Noah's day and in Lot's day. Just as surely as we know that God destroyed everyone outside the Ark and everyone inside Sodom and Gomorrah, we know that He will return, and when He does return, one of the first things He will do is judge.

Matthew 24:40-42
Then shall two be in the field; the one shall be taken, and the other left.

Two women shall be grinding at the mill; the one shall be taken, and the other left.

Watch therefore: for ye know not what hour your Lord doth come.

As soon as Jesus returns, one of the first things He will do is judge. He alludes to that when He speaks of one being taken and the other left. The one that is taken is taken to be judged, and that is not a good thing. This particular judgment is not a judgment for the righteous. It is a judgment for the unrighteous. Those who are judged will unfortunately be killed, and their spirit sent to hell.

Do you remember the reference to *"wheresoever the carcase is, there will the eagles be gathered together"*? Jesus said that in Matthew 24:28 and He means that the judgment upon His return will result in the deaths of many. Their bodies will die and pile up and the birds of prey like eagles will feed on them.

This judgment is for those who do not know Jesus, who are not in relationship with Him. It is for those who have either never made a decision about Jesus, or those who have outwardly rejected Him as being Savior and Lord. Those who reject Him, He will reject. That is tragic, but it is fully avoidable. Anyone can trust Jesus for salvation, thereby becoming born again and entering into a relationship with Him. Anyone, including you.

Matthew 24:43-44
But know this, that if the goodman of the house had known in what watch the thief would come, he would have watched, and would not have suffered his house to be broken up.

Therefore be ye also ready: for in such an hour as ye think not the Son of man cometh.

Before Jesus speaks of the coming judgment, He takes the time to emphasize the fact that people who know when something is going to happen normally prepare for it. We see this all the time in society.

If people have an advance warning of a tornado, they do what they can to protect themselves. If they have a storm cellar, they head there. If they do not, they go to a part of the house that they believe will offer them the most protection from the coming storm.

If a person believes that for one reason or another their home or car is going to be broken into, they normally take precautions against it. This is simply common sense.

If people believe that their wealth opens them up to potential kidnappings or other dangers, they hire body guards to decrease the chances of something bad happening to them. To not take these types of precautions would be ludicrous.

No one leaves their house today, goes on a trip, and leaves their home unlocked or their garage door wide open. They are simply inviting trouble. Most people have more than one lock on their doors, have extra locks on their windows, and some even go so far as to have an alarm system installed or a security company on retainer. People do this because they understand the element of danger that exists in society. The most we can say is that some areas of society have less of a crime problem than other areas, but there is no place that is virtually free of crime. As long as fallen human beings live on this planet (and that is everyone), crime and evil will exist.

Jesus is urging His listeners to recognize that signs provide a warning that something will happen soon. To ignore the signs is to ignore the danger. Too many people go through this life with their heads in the sand, preferring to not think of problems in society. As long as those problems do not affect them, things are fine. Evil can happen anywhere. No one is immune, not even Christians.

Matthew 24:45-51
Who then is a faithful and wise servant, whom his lord hath made ruler over his household, to give them meat in due season?

Blessed is that servant, whom his lord when he cometh shall find so doing.

Verily I say unto you, That he shall make him ruler over all his goods.

But and if that evil servant shall say in his heart, My lord delayeth his coming;

And shall begin to smite his fellowservants, and to eat and drink with the drunken;

The lord of that servant shall come in a day when he looketh not for him, and in an hour that he is not aware of,

And shall cut him asunder, and appoint him his portion with the hypocrites: there shall be weeping and gnashing of teeth.

Jesus ends His discourse while on the Mt. of Olives with an illustration that further brings out the truth of the basis of judgment. In this illustration, Jesus compares two types of servants. The first one is a good servant because he cares for those people that the Lord has put in his charge. Do not take this to mean that this refers only to pastors or teachers of the Bible. It refers to everyone.

There are two types of people in this illustration, and the one is clearly good, while the other is clearly evil. They are distinguished by what they do and how they care for others. The first servant does not cheat people. He is honest, caring, and gives people what they need in order to be healthy. Being healthy here is not simply being physically healthy. It is also being spiritually healthy.

There are some today who believe that being a Christian means doing the things that Jesus did by making people's lives physically better or easier. Their emphasis is on taking care of the sick, the homeless, or visiting those in prison.

These are all good things. Unfortunately, none of these things will save a person. If I never share my testimony with anyone, if I never tell them how to become born again, or saved, I have not fully "fed" people. I have not given them meat in due season.

While it is needed and wonderful to give people the things that make their lives physically better, if we stop there, we have cheated them. It is our obligation as Christians to teach people how to become saved, in order that they will be given eternal life. Without eternal life, no amount of physical niceties in this life amount to anything.

The good servant gives people what they need in the physical realm, and most importantly, directs these same people to look to Jesus as Savior and Lord. The people who only focus on the physical needs and yet ignore the spiritual are stealing. They are holding back from giving them the most important "meat" available.

This is what the evil servant does. He does not care about the spiritual needs of people. He may even abuse them by not providing for their physical needs. He certainly abuses them spiritually by not teaching them how to become born again. That is the evil servant, and because of that, that servant will be judged.

Let me also state that this illustration is not teaching that good works save a person. The first servant – the good one – represents the person who is authentically saved. He is a true Christian and treats others as Jesus would treat them. Because the first servant is truly and authentically saved, he also wants others to be saved, and so is very willing to share the gospel with them in the hopes that God will open their eyes to the truth, just as He opened the eyes of the thief on the cross (cf. Luke 23:42-43). Once the thief's eyes were opened by God, He saw the truth about Jesus and responded to Him by *embracing* that truth. Once He embraced that truth, he also wound up embracing salvation.

The evil servant is called a hypocrite by Jesus, and for good reason. While he talked the talk, he did not walk the walk. People who call themselves Christians should have lives that measure up. No, they will not be perfect in this life, because the sin nature continues with us until we die. Once we die, the sin nature is removed and we receive a nature that is fully unable to ever sin again.

11

HYPOCRISY

Those who call themselves Christians but are not Christians will wind up living lives that consistently shows them to be hypocrites. They will have secret lives in which they indulge their secret sins. As long as these sins are kept hidden from people, they believe that no one sees. If no one sees, they will continue to live a double life, showing the public one face, while in secret, their private lives are something else entirely.

We have seen this repeatedly throughout society. Well known ministers or evangelists are caught up in illicit affairs or worse, and it finally becomes known to the public. As it turns out, they may have been doing what they did in private for years, yet they stood on the platform every Sunday to condemn sin and those who were involved in it. This hypocrisy will find them out, and what they do in private will be seen in public.

A number of years ago, a friend, who had a really jovial personality, knew of my Christianity. He was not a Christian as far as I could tell and his own verbal testimony told me that he had rejected it. For him, life was good and there was always something to kid about.

He had long ago dealt with the concept of Christianity. He shared with me that he was filling up his gas tank one Sunday when another car pulled up just across from his so that he could see the person and into his car. It turned out to be a minister from the area who was there to refill his gas tank.

They chatted briefly and when it came time to pay for the gas, my friend noticed the minister rip open one of the offering envelopes that people use to place their money in during the offertory. The minister then proceeded to simply remove the cash from the envelope and pay for his gas.

Was the minister stealing? Quite possibly. Certainly, he might have written down the amount on the envelope so that the accountant would know how much had been in the envelope. However, my friend had a point. It seemed clear enough that this minister took what did not necessarily belong to him and used it for his own personal needs. It may not be as cut and dry as that, but the reality is that what the minister did *appeared* to my friend to be fully hypocritical. He had a point. That minister may well have been hypocritical.

However, my friend also missed a very important point. Just because someone says they are a Christian, or makes their living as a pastor, minister, teacher, or missionary, it does not mean that they are actually born again. It does not mean that they are truly and authentically saved.

My friend rejected Christianity based on the hypocrisy of that minister. At the very least, the minister should have been far more careful about opening those envelopes and using the money, even if he had the right to do so. He should have realized how his actions might look to those around him. In this case, he caused my friend to doubt and reject Christianity.

A number of years later, my friend died very unexpectedly. If he ever changed his mind about Christianity, I never knew of it. In that case, he went into eternity through the door of death with the same attitude and belief toward Christianity he'd had for some time. Take a moment to reflect on what he saw immediately after his death, if the Bible is true.

If the Bible is true, my friend saw God, and he instantly became aware of the truth of the Bible. Here he was seeing it, and because of that he could no longer ignore it or reject it. He was faced with the fact that he now knew Christianity to be true, though he had rejected it while he lived.

The problem of course is that if that is the way my friend went into eternity, it was too late to change his mind. His decision, like yours, must be made here, in this lifetime. You cannot put it off because you think you will deal with it later on. That day – later on – may never arrive.

WHAT ABOUT YOU?

Do you know when you will die? Are you aware of the day and hour when you will slip from this life into eternity? I bet you do not know when that will happen. So why are you living as if you **do** *know when it will happen?* Putting a decision about Jesus off until another day is taking a huge chance because of the fact that you do not know when you will die. That is plainly simple, and logic alone demands that you do not put this decision off. Yet you do, because the thought of becoming a Christian makes you feel uncomfortable.

You wrongly believe that to become a Christian means that you have to change in a major way *before* Jesus will accept you. It means to you giving up the things you love now because if you love them, then obviously they are wrong and God does not love them.

You are putting the cart before the horse. You must understand that God is not rejecting you. He is not standing there, tapping His foot demanding that you eliminate those things that He does not like before you can come to Him for salvation.

If you (or anyone) could do that, you would not *need* His salvation at all. It is because you and I do things that are not pleasing to Him that we need His salvation.

What do you do that you would like to no longer do? Do you drink excessively until you cannot control it? Do you play around with drugs? Do you eat too much food until you have become overweight, lethargic and sickly?

What other things are in your life that you do not like? Are you drawn to illicit extra-marital affairs? Do you have a problem with lust? Are you a shopaholic? Do you tend to tell lies a great deal because it makes you feel important, or to hide things about your life?

Do you find that you do not like people and you would prefer to be around animals or out in the woods than around people? Are you a workaholic? Do you place a high value on money and you find that you work very hard to obtain it?

Here's the problem. The enemy of our souls comes to us and tells us that God will never accept us until we get rid of those things. He lies to us that God essentially wants us "perfect" before He will be willing to meet us and grant us eternal life. This is completely untrue.

The other lie that our enemy tells us is that we should not become a Christian because the fun in our life will fly out the door. We will no longer be able to drink or do the fun things we enjoy now. We start to think that coming to God means becoming a doormat for people and having to fill our life with things we do not want to *ever* do.

These are all lies, and unfortunately, too many people believe them. First of all, God does not expect you to be "perfect" before you come to Him for salvation. If that were the case, no one would be able to ever approach Him.

Secondly, God does not say that He is going to take away all the things we enjoy and replace them with things we hate. What is wrong with enjoying the lake on your boat? What is wrong with spending a day with the family fishing or just relaxing in the mountains? There is nothing wrong with these things.

What God *will* do is begin to remove the things that have ensnared you so that life is actually draining from you, but you are not aware of it. For instance, maybe you drink excessively and you have tried everything you can think of to quit. You have gone to AA meetings, spent thousands of dollars on this program or that, and you have even used your own will power to free yourself from the addiction to alcohol, all to no avail.

The question is not: *do I need to quit before I come to Jesus*? The question is: *am I willing to allow Him to work in and through me to take away the addiction I have to alcohol*? Do you see the difference? Are you willing to allow Him to work in you to break that addiction so that you will become a healthier person, one who is able to think straight and one who learns to rely on Him for strength? That is all He wants you to be able to do. He knows you cannot break that addiction (or any addiction for that matter) with your own strength and willpower. Are you willing to allow Him to do it in and through you?

What if you are a workaholic? What if you have "things" like a boat, a house in Cancun, a large bank account, four cars, and more? Do you think that God is going to ask you to give it up, or worse, do you think that God will simply come in and take all of that from you? I know of nothing in Scripture that tells us He will do that.

What God will do with all of those who come to Him trusting Him for salvation is one thing, which begins the moment we receive salvation and will continue until the day we stand before Him. He will begin to create within us the character of Jesus (cf. Ephesians 2:10).

Here is a verse from the Old Testament that was said originally through the prophet Ezekiel to the people of Israel. While this was specifically stated to the Jews, it is applicable to all who receive salvation through Jesus Christ.

"I will give you a new heart and put a new spirit within you; I will take the heart of stone out of your flesh and give you a heart of flesh. I will put My Spirit within you and cause you to walk in My statutes, and you will keep My judgments and do them" (Ezekiel 36:26-27).

God is speaking here through Ezekiel, and He is saying that He will give the people a new heart of flesh, removing that old heart of stone. This is God's responsibility. God is the One who makes that happen. We are told in the book of Hebrews that God is the Author and Finisher of our faith (cf. Hebrews 12:2). This tells me that God is the One who changes me from within so that over time, my desires are slowly turned into His desires.

I recall years ago thinking that God wanted to do everything in my life that I did not want Him to do. I fell into the asinine belief that He wanted to change everything about me. What I learned is that yes, there are things that God does want to change about me. However, there is a lot that God originally gave me that He has also enhanced and used for His glory.

Maybe you are a workaholic who thinks that working hard is something God does not want you to do. This is not necessarily the case.

He may have given you the ability and the knowledge to work in the area of finance for a great purpose. All He may wind up doing is dialing back your workaholic tendencies so that you have more time to enjoy your family and study His Word.

But you say you smoke, or drink, or use illegal drugs and you don't want to give those up. As I stated, you can't give those up under your own power, and the fact that you have tried so many times has proven it to you.

But God knows what is and what is not good for you. Are you willing to *allow* Him to work in you to change your desires so that you no longer want to smoke, use illegal drugs, or drink nearly as much?

Then you say that you believe God wants to make you a Christian so you can become miserable. Isn't that what most Christians are; miserable? Not the Christians I know, and certainly not me, my wife, or our children.

Where does the Bible say that God wants us miserable? You will not find it. What God wants is for us to be blessed, and that begins when we receive salvation from His hand.

You know, if we would stop and take the time to consider the fact that this life is exceedingly short if we compare it to eternity, we will then realize that there is nothing so important that it should keep us from receiving Jesus as Savior and Lord.

Unfortunately, too many people do not consider the brevity of life. They think they will live forever, or at the very least, they will die when they are really old and gray. That will come too soon. This author is going to be 54 years old in just a few months from this writing. It truly seems like yesterday that I was a young boy fishing in the Delaware River near Hobart, New York. There I spent many Saturdays fishing and simply enjoying being outdoors. How did life go by so very quickly? How could that have happened?

It has happened and I am at a point in life where not only do I realize that this life is short, but I actually look forward to spending eternity with Jesus after this life. Does that sound morbid to you? It shouldn't, because by comparing this life to eternity, we should get a sense of what is truly important.

God does not expect us to become Mother Theresas. He does not necessarily expect us to give up everything and become missionaries in outer Mongolia. What God expects is for us to simply allow Him to change our character as He sees fit.

Over time, we may well find that we have simply stopped swearing without realizing it. Our desire for cigarettes or alcohol has nearly evaporated. Illicit affairs no longer enter the picture.

We also may find that some of the things we want to eliminate in our life become more pronounced. Often the enemy will do this to cause us to focus on something that God is not even doing in our lives at that point. It causes tension, frustration, and self-anger.

If you have gotten to this point in your life and you have not dealt with the question about Jesus, it is about time you do so. You need to stop what you are doing and realize a couple of things before you go through another minute in this life.

- **Sinner**: you need to realize that you are a sinner. You have sinned and you will continue to sin. Sin is breaking the laws that God has set up. We all sin. We have all broken God's laws and that breaks any connection we might have had with God. Sin pushes us away from Him.

    Romans 3:23 says *"For all have sinned, and come short of the glory of God."* That means you and that means me. All means all. That is the first step. We need to recognize and agree with God that yes, we are sinners. I'm a sinner. You are a sinner. This results in God's anger, what the Bible terms "wrath."

- **God's Wrath**: Romans 1:18 says, *"For the wrath of God is revealed from heaven against all ungodliness and unrighteousness of men, who suppress the truth in unrighteousness."*

This is as much a fact as the truth that we are all sinners. Because we are sinners – by breaking God's law(s) – God has every right to be angry with us and ultimately destroy that which is sinful. If we choose to remain "in" our sinful states throughout this life, we will – unfortunately – be destroyed with the rest of sin.

Fortunately, there *is* a remedy, and it is salvation.

- **God's Gift**: In the sixteenth chapter of Acts, a jailer asks Paul this famous question: *what must I do to be saved?* The question was asked because Paul and Barnabas had been imprisoned, and while there, they began singing praises to God.

God then sent a powerful earthquake that opened the doors to all the prison cells, yet no one escaped. When the jailer arrived, he saw that everyone was still in their cells. and after seeing that miracle (what prisoner would not want to escape from prison?), turned and asked what he must do to be saved. He was speaking of the spiritual aspect of things. He wanted to know how he could be guaranteed eternal life.

The answer Paul gave the man was, *"Believe on the Lord Jesus Christ, and thou shalt be saved, and thy house"* (Acts 16:31).

This is not head knowledge or intellectual assent. This is *believing from the heart.* In fact, Paul makes a very similar statement in another book he wrote, Romans. He says, *"That if thou shalt confess with thy mouth the Lord Jesus, and shalt believe in thine heart that God hath raised him from the dead, thou shalt be saved. For with the heart man believeth unto righteousness; and with the mouth confession is made unto salvation"* (Romans 10:9-10).

When we fully believe something, we confess that it is true. It must begin in the heart because that is where the will is located. We must want to believe. We must endeavor to believe. We must seek to believe.

We must stop giving ourselves all the reasons to deny or ignore Jesus. As God, He became a Man, born of a virgin. He clothed Himself with humanity that He might show us how to live, and in so doing, would keep every portion of the law.

If Jesus was capable of keeping every portion of the law, then He would be found worthy to become a sacrifice for our sin – yours and mine. If He became a sacrifice for our sin, then all that we must do is embrace Him and His sacrificial death.

In short then, to become saved we must:

1. Admit (we sin)
2. Repent (want to turn away from it)
3. Believe (that Jesus is the answer)
4. Embrace (the truth about Jesus)

We **admit** that we are sinner, that we have sinned. This is nothing more than agreeing with God that we have broken His law. Can you honestly say that you have not broken God's law? If you admit to breaking even the "smallest" law, then you are a lawbreaker.

After we admit that we have sinned, the next step is found in **repenting**. Some believe that repenting is actually moving away from sin. This author believes that it is a willingness to move away from sin, and there is a difference.

As we have already discussed, it is impossible to stop sinning. Human beings simply cannot do it because as long as we live, we will have a sin nature, which is something within us that gives us a propensity to sin. As long as we have this inner propensity to sin or break God's laws, we will never be perfect in this life.

We cannot one day say "Lord, I promise to stop sinning." If we do that, we are only kidding ourselves and setting ourselves up for major failure. We cannot stop sinning in this life. The most we can do is *want* to stop sinning and then spend the rest of our lives allowing God to create the character of Jesus within us, slowly, little by little.

Repenting is to decide that you no longer want to do the things that keep us out of heaven. We no longer wish to break God's laws. It is not promising God that we will never sin again.

Once we admit, then repent, we must **believe**. This is one of the most difficult things to do because believing that Jesus died in our place, that He lived a perfectly sinless life, is extremely difficult to believe. Our minds cannot grasp that truth. We must ask God to open our eyes to that truth so that we can embrace it.

While on the cross next to Jesus, the one thief joined the other thief in ridiculing Jesus. Then, all of a sudden – as we read in Luke 23 – this same thief that had just been ridiculing Him now turned to Him with a new understanding.

It was this new understanding that prompted the thief to say to Jesus, *"Lord, remember me when you come into your Kingdom."* Jesus looked at the man and responded to him, *"Today, you will be with me in paradise."*

What had occurred in the mind and heart of that thief from one moment to the next? One thing, and that one thing was that God opened the thief's eyes so that he could see the truth. It was as if the blinders fell off and he now saw and understood who Jesus was, even to the most cursory degree that Jesus was dying not for Himself, but for others.

It was this understanding, this awareness, which prompted the man to ask Jesus to simply be remembered. Jesus went way beyond it to promise the man that he would be with Jesus that day in paradise.

Please notice in Luke 23 that there is nothing in the chapter that tells us that the man promised Jesus he would give up sin, or that he would never sin again. There is nothing that tells us that thief took the time to enter into a final deathbed confession of his sins so that he could be absolved.

The thief made no promises to Jesus at all. What he experienced was the truth of who Jesus was and what Jesus accomplished for humanity. Jesus accomplished what we cannot. What is left is for each person to *admit, repent, believe,* and *embrace.*

Let me clarify here that though we do not see any verbal repentance from the thief, we know that he did repent. He admitted as well. How can we know this? Because of the thief's complete about-face with respect to his attitude toward Jesus. One minute, he was ridiculing Jesus, and the next, embracing Him. This is important. There is no way he could have or would have *embraced* Jesus had he not been humbled by the truth *about* Jesus.

Once the thief saw the truth, he was instantly humbled. Within himself, he knew that he was a sinner, and in fact the text states that this is what he told the other thief dying next to him. *"But the other answering rebuked him, saying, Dost not thou fear God, seeing thou art in the same condemnation? And we indeed justly; for we receive the due reward of our deeds: but this man hath done nothing amiss*" (Luke 23:40-41). Something happened within the heart of the one thief. In one moment, the thief went from harassing Jesus to recognizing his own sinfulness, and then ultimately, asking for grace, which was freely given to him.

Whether he said it or not, the thief went from haughtiness to humility in a very short space of time, and it was all because he saw the truth about Jesus. That truth helped him realize that he deserved his death and what would happen to him after death. He understood that Jesus did not deserve death.

From here, the thief fully embraced the truth about Jesus and was rewarded with eternal life because of it. He did not come off the cross to be water baptized. He did not list a long litany of offenses against God. He recognized the truth about Jesus, was humbled, and embraced that truth!

This is what each of us needs to do. We cannot give in to the lie that tells us that we are not good enough, or we have not given up enough before God will accept us. We must reject the lie that says we must somehow earn our salvation.

Jesus has done everything that is necessary to make salvation available to us. The only thing that is left for us is to see the truth. Once we see that truth, it should humble us to the point of embracing Jesus and all that He stands for and is to us.

The eighth chapter of Romans begins with the fact that all who trust Jesus for salvation are no longer condemned...*ever*. All of my sins – past, present, and future – have not only been forgiven, but canceled. It is because of my faith in the atonement (death) of Jesus that God is able to cancel all of my sins, even the ones that I have not committed yet. This does not make me eager to commit them. It makes me want to do what I can to avoid sinning.

If you do not know Jesus, please do not put down this book without deliberately *believing* that He is God, that He died for you by the shedding of His blood on the cross, and that He rose three days later because death could not keep Him. Do you believe that? If you do not yet believe it, do you *want* to believe it? If so, then simply ask God to help you come to believe all that Jesus is and all that He has accomplished for you. God will answer your prayers and you may either receive instantaneous awareness of all that Jesus is and has done, or it may be a *growing* awareness over time. In either case, it is the most important decision you will ever make.

Turn to Him now and pray for knowledge of the truth and an ability to embrace it. Please. He is waiting for you.

Ask Yourself:

1. Do you *know* Jesus? Are you in *relationship* with Him? Have you had a spiritual transaction according to John 3?
2. Do you *want* to receive eternal life through the only salvation that is available?
3. Do you believe that Jesus is God the Son, who was born of a virgin, lived a sinless life, died a bloody and gruesome death to pay for your sin, was buried, and rose again on the third day? Do you *believe* this?
4. Do you *want* to *embrace* the truth from #3?
5. Pray that God will open your eyes and provide you with the faith to begin believing the truth about Jesus. Ask Him to help your faith embrace the truth, realizing that you are not good enough to save yourself and that your sin will keep you out of God's Kingdom without His salvation.
6. Pray as if your life depended upon it because *it does*!
7. If you have prayed to receive Jesus as Savior and Lord, please write to me. I want to send you some materials at *no charge or obligation*. Write to me at **fred_deruvo@hotmail.com** and sign up for our free bimonthly newsletter at **www.studygrowknow.com**

Listen to our radio program, **Study-Grow-Know,** on the following stations:

- **AM950 KAHI** or listen on their Website **www.kahi.com** Saturdays at Noon
- **Live365.com** and search for Study-Grow-Know

All of our programs are archived at our own Web site **www.studygrowknow.com** on our **BLOG** page from the MENU

  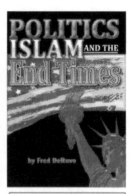

www.studygrowknow.com or wherever quality books are sold!

We are looking up, Deb!

Made in the USA
Charleston, SC
25 February 2011